WEAVING WITHOUT A LOOM

Weaving
WITHOUT A LOOM

SECOND EDITION

Sarita R. Rainey
Art Educator, Author

Davis Publications Inc.
Worcester, Massachusetts

Publisher: Wyatt Wade
Managing Editor: David Coen
Project Editor: Reba Libby
Manufacturing Coordinator: Georgiana Rock
Editors: Claire Mowbray Golding, Janet Stone
Photo research: AR Photo Research
Editorial assistants: Annette Cinelli, Missy Nicholson
Design and production: Janis Owens, Books By Design, Inc.

ISBN: 978-0-87192-785-9

1 2 3 4 5 6 7 8 9 10   13 14 15 12 11 10 09 08 07
Printed in Canada

Credits
Front cover: Clockwise from **top left**: Collection of the author (see page 6); **top right**: James Mosier and Wendy Benard, *Woven Aluminum Vessel* (see page 119). **Lower left**: Honma Kazuaki, *Sound of Waves II*, 2000. Hobichiku and kurochiku bamboos, using Mage and hineri-ami technique (see page 119); **lower right**: Collection of the author (see page 118). Back cover: **Top**: Angela Bangrazi, *The Old Woman Who Swallowed a Fly* (see page 95); **bottom**: Raffia weaving (see page 104).

Title page: Traditional basket, Eritrea, Africa. © Frances Linzee Gordon/Getty Images

CONTENTS

INTRODUCTION

The first interlocking of twisted fibers to make fabric was a major development in the history of humankind. Early weavings were made without complicated mechanical looms or extensive preparation. They were fabricated with natural materials and minimal equipment. There is renewed interest in these early off-loom techniques, which offer enormous versatility and creative opportunity.

As *Weaving Without a Loom* illustrates, threads can be put under tension with simple equipment—a picture frame, a piece of cardboard, a pencil. Whereas the traditional floor loom can be impersonal, more basic tools enable the artist to use free weaving techniques to create expressive new forms and constructions. In some instances, such as weaving on a forked tree branch, the weaving equipment becomes an integral part of the finished work.

In addition to fundamental tools, this book explores a variety of everyday items that can be used for textile construction. Materials take on a new role with unconventional combinations of fiber with metal, paper, wood, wire, nylon, plastic, and rope.

The off-loom approach to weaving offers distinct advantages. Unrestricted by the painstaking procedures and complicated equipment of conventional loom weaving, the artist is free to experiment. In addition to being accessible, inexpensive, simple, and portable, this approach enables ease of construction, spontaneity, and flexibility of design and structure. Basic methods and uncomplicated equipment can be used in elementary projects and more complex constructions. They can be used to create functional items or purely expressive artworks.

Dr. Rainey, an art educator and author of a variety of books on fiber art, has used these off-loom techniques in her own work. She has exhibited at the Smithsonian in Washington, DC, the Contemporary Crafts Museum in New York City, and at other museums around the United States. As an art educator, she has experience at all levels of teaching, elementary through adult education.

In this book she encourages exploration of age-old techniques to create exciting new forms. It is an important source for the creation of imaginative and innovative fiber art.

Cassandra Lee Tellier, Ph.D.
Director, The Schumacher Gallery
Capital University
Columbus, Ohio

1

WEAVING AS AN Art Form

Loom from Rimac or Lurin Valley, Peru. © Erich Lessing/Art Resource, NY

(opposite) Navajo weaving on a primitive loom. Courtesy American Museum of Natural History. ©Ray Manley/Superstock

Weaving is usually defined as the interweaving of threads. As an art form, however, it is much more than this. It is a means of creative expression which allows an imaginative person to recapture the thrill of creativity that the primitive weaver once knew.

Weaving has been, since primitive times, a medium for the artist as well as for the person faced with the practical problem of producing cloth, and in every period of history, both types of weaving have been practiced.

Human beings first wove a few threads together with the only tools available to them—their fingers. With these they lifted different combinations of warp strands and inserted the weft between the separated warp fibers. They intertwined fibers of various textures to produce patterns and used color to breathe life into them. Inevitably, new materials led to more sophisticated designs, glowing with exotic color and pulsating with life.

As they developed their skills, early weavers sought to speed the weaving process. Instead of using their fingers to raise each thread, they discovered that they could insert a rod under certain threads and raise all of them at one time. By using more than one rod, they found that they could form patterns even faster.

Step by step, the loom continued to evolve and become more complex. A device called the harness was invented to raise and lower the warp threads automatically. Complicated power looms appeared, and primitive tools were put away to gather dust.

However, primitive weaving methods still survive among some crafters in the United States and other countries. In an era of discovery,

Model of a Greek loom. Weights are attached to warp to hold the fibers in place. Photo by Rene Hatzenbichler. Courtesy Michael Lahanas; www.hlahanas.de

weaving without the popular but impersonal harness loom offers new excitement and challenge. Those who seek to rediscover the simplicity of this primitive art may use a simple frame or background material instead of the harness loom. It is with these and other devices that this book is concerned. Specifically, this book aims to minimize weaving terminology as it explains warp and weft usage; offer weaving variations; expand perception; develop a creative approach with methods and materials; and provide weaving examples for inspiration at all age levels. The devices have been selected on the basis of their simplicity and will enable you and your students to develop a personal approach to weaving.

The weaving process can provide a challenge to the imaginative artist, stimulating discriminating decisions in the use of color, texture, and shape; and expanding perceptions beyond method and technique to the aesthetic. This book illustrates how creative and imaginative weaving on the simplest device provides a challenge to fuse ideas, material, and function into an aesthetic whole.

Egyptian weaving shop, Middle Kingdom. Found near El Giza, Upper Egypt. © Werner Forman/Art Resource, NY

THE WEAVING PROCESS

Weaving, simply defined, is the interlacing of threads at right angles to each other. The **warp** threads are the vertical threads that make the structural "skeleton" for weaving. The **weft** threads are the horizontal fibers woven through the warp. **Warp and weft control the design.**

Warp threads are vertical; **weft** threads are horizontal.

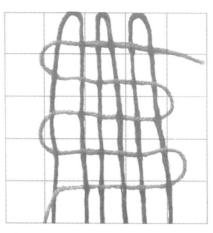

Threads interlaced at right angles.

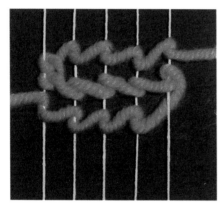

Wrapping yarn around warp threads creates interesting effects.

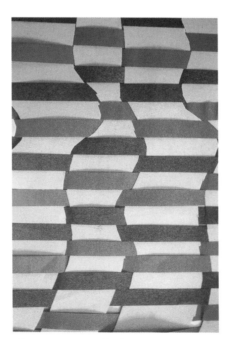

The **warp** controls the design in this example.

Here the **weft** controls the design.

The **design** of the weaving is determined by color, texture, space, line, shape, and rhythm. No one of these stands alone; all work together to form a harmonious whole.

Color can be used to inspire, motivate, accent, set moods, and evoke atmosphere. **Textures** can be rough, smooth, soft, or hard.

Thick, thin, wide, or narrow **lines** are used for direction, movement, or accent. **Space** can be negative or positive, open or closed. **Form**, the outside shape of the weaving, can be used to provide an outline, which might then be filled in; multiple forms might interlock or overlap a central figure. **Rhythm** is the repetition of color, line, shape, or texture that creates a feeling of movement.

Inspiration for weaving may come from a variety of sources, including the environment (people, animals, nature), the designs around you, and the many materials you can use to weave.

Varied **textures** create visual interest.

Interlocking **shapes** and threads give these woven forms a feeling of movement.

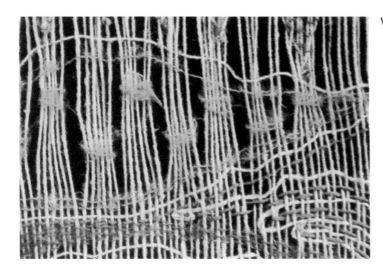

Woven **lines** can be straight or meandering.

Uneven edges and a weaving's outer shape can create unexpected **spaces**.

Negative (open) and **positive** (closed) **space** give weavings dynamism.

2

WEAVING WITH Paper

BASIC MATERIALS
construction paper of various colors
poster paper
scissors
stapler
glue or glue sticks

Optional Materials
X-acto knife
single-edge razor blade
tag board of various colors
heavy white paper

Let's experiment with weaving without a loom. All you need is some imagination and the most readily available material—**paper**. Paper can be a challenge to the ingenuity of any designer-weaver, encouraging endless variations in choice of color, texture, line, and pattern.

Many types of paper may be used for weaving—cellophanes, crepe, metallic, tissue, glazed, blotting, velour, gift, shelf, and wallpapers. Colorful tag boards, paper ribbons, tapes, and even everyday newspaper are also effective. Papers can be found in scrap piles or purchased from gift wrapping departments, paper companies, and hardware, wallpaper, or stationery stores.

Collect papers for a period of time before you start weaving. Look for colorful and textured papers to stimulate your imagination and inspire ideas. Interesting weaving patterns can be made by using assorted colored papers that range from pastel orchids and pinks to brilliant purples and reds, or by combining rough, smooth, shiny, and dull papers.

Paper weaving can start in kindergarten and proceed through college, each level contributing new and exciting complexities to the craft. The basic operations involved in cutting and weaving warp and weft serve to familiarize beginners with the weaving process and to develop their appreciation for a simple weaving technique. Advanced students can discover more intricate and aesthetic designs by further varying the way warp and weft are cut, varying the way strips of paper are woven, and combining paper weaving with techniques such as block printing and paper sculpture.

(above and left) Cut an animal shape and make slits in it. Weave paper strips through the slits. Placing the animal shape on a slightly larger piece of contrasting paper adds visual interest.

(opposite) Human figures, silhouetted and created in two colors of construction paper, were woven in and out of thin vertical strips. This technique is called *shaped weft*.

PROCEDURE

There are a number of ways to cut a sheet of paper so that strips can be woven into it. Vertically cut strips act as warp, while horizontal strips are the weft. Here is an easy method for cutting warp:

- Fold a sheet of paper in half.
- Rule a line across the paper about ½″ (1.3 cm) down from the open edges to serve as the margin at top and bottom when opened.
- Cut strips of equal or unequal widths, stopping at the margin.

Margins at the top and bottom of the warp help hold the weaving together. Only the top margin is visible here, as the paper is folded.

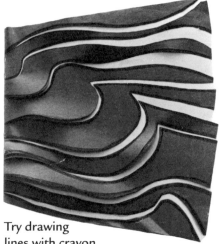

Try drawing lines with crayon and cutting along the lines to create an irregular warp.

Weave through the cut strips.

This method may be easier for young children:

- On a flat sheet of paper, make a warp by marking the margin at the top edge.
- Cut strips to that margin.
- Pass the weft, the strip of paper used for weaving, under and over the warp, gluing each strip at the end to hold it in place.

- Alternating the strips, so that one strip goes over the warp while the other goes under, will make a tabby pattern and will further hold the weaving together.

Remember, there are unlimited possibilities for design in paper weaving.

This simple warp has only a top margin. To give the weaving body, glue each strip of weft in place after weaving it through the warp.

Even a pattern that appears complicated may be simple to make.

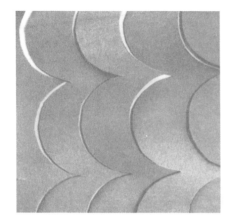

Cut paper to form the warp.

Cut slanted slits into a strip of paper. Then weave another strip of paper through the slits.

Weave each combined strip as though it were one.

The finished work has a complex visual pattern.

VARIATIONS

Warp and Weft Experiments

To add variety and interest to paper weaving, try these experiments with warp and weft.

Make the warp control the design. Cut strips into shapes, then weave through them. For example, cut curved or angular warp strips; vary the width of the warp strips for interesting patterns; cut shapes out of, or into, the warp from one or both edges. Then weave straight strips through the irregular warp.

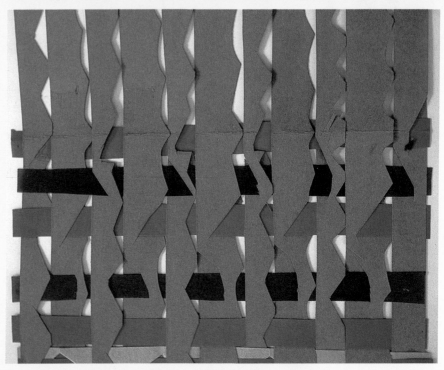

Cut warp to form irregular shapes; weave straight strips through them.

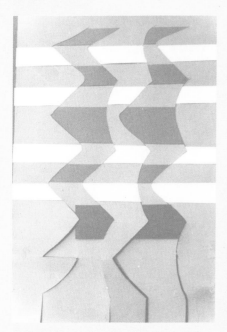

Cut angles and curves to form varied warp strips.

Try very wide warp strips.

Make the weft control the design. Weave over and under different combinations of strips. For example, weave over one, under two, over three, under two, or over one, and under three; cut parts out of the weft; shape the weft by cutting angular, jagged, or curved lines. Weave narrower strips of contrasting colors over previously woven weft.

Try weaving over and under an irregular number of strips.

Repeat a complex cut weft to make a background for the warp.

Zigzag shapes cut into the weft create a striking pattern.

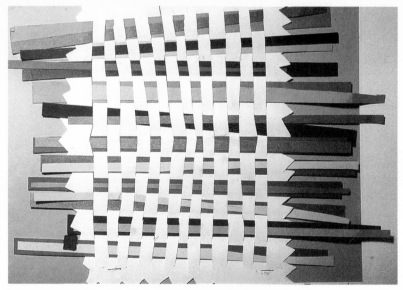

Add narrow strips of contrasting colors to an already-woven weft. Student work, grade 1.

Irregular cut warp with straight weft strips.

Use torn paper strips for warp and weft.

A dark, irregular warp contrasts with a light-colored, straight weft.

Surface Enrichments

Paper weaving, whether simple or intricate, must have a pleasing and well-organized design before you add surface enrichments. Basic weaving principles, sensitivity to design, and careful use of materials are essential to the success of any variation. Here are some of many possible ways to enrich your weaving:

- Glue a narrow strip of contrasting color on top of the weft before using it for weaving.
- Glue interesting flat or sculptured shapes on top of the squares or rectangles formed by the weaving design.
- Apply shapes of color and printed text from magazines over certain areas of the weaving, making a collage effect.
- Weave a form, such as an animal, over and into the tabby design, leaving part of the tabby weave for background.
- Punch holes through the weaving, using a paper punch, then superimpose the weaving over a contrasting paper.
- Use paint, crayon, yarn, string, or fabric to accent certain woven areas.
- Create Op Art designs by drawing optical line patterns, then cutting along those lines to form an intricate warp.

(above) Paste paper shapes on both warp and weft before and after weaving, to add visual interest.

Tie paper around paper strips for a sculptural look.

Weave folded strips over and under straight strips to create a three-dimensional effect. Courtesy of Eileen Scally.

Optical Patterns

Weave "rays" from a central circular shape into a straight warp. Weave weft strips of differing widths.

Create Op Art effects by using contrasting colors and various shaped paper strips.

Weaving as Accent

Weaving can add interest to simple cutout figures.

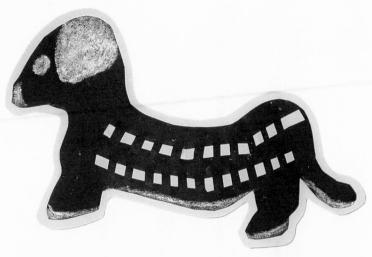

Use crayons or oil pastels to add details to cutout figures.

This warp was cut in vertical zigzag lines. Straight strips of paper were woven horizontally through it.

This shape was outlined in yarn. Yarn weaving was used to accent the body of the figure.

These figures were first drawn in crayon on construction paper. They were then cut out, and horizontal or vertical slits were cut into them. Contrasting paper strips were woven through the slits.

Shaped Warp

A shaped warp allows you to create larger areas of flat color within a woven design, and gives you the opportunity to make woven works that are irregular and freeform. To create a shaped warp, make a ½" (1.3 cm) margin around the paper.

Draw a shape that touches the top, bottom, and sides of the margin. Cut away the negative space around the shape. Cut intricate designs out of the weft strips or paste shapes onto the strips to add interest to the weaving.

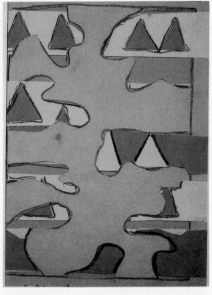

Cut and glue paper shapes to strips of paper. Outline the basic shapes in crayon or oil pastel before and after weaving.

A shape that touches the margin on all sides will give body and strength to the shape or warp.

Weave strips of paper over and under the shape that serves as a warp. Cut designs in these weft strips if you like.

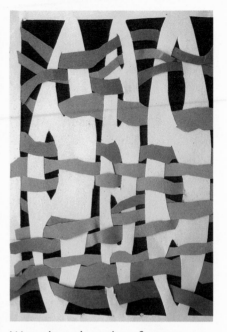

Weave irregular strips of paper through a shaped paper warp.

Outlining shapes and edges in different oil pastel colors creates additional movement in the weaving.

Circle Warp

Circle warps appear to have been made by magic unless you know the process. Experiment with different ways of cutting and tearing the warp and you'll be surprised by some of the visual effects.

To make this paper weaving, cut V-shapes for the warp into a sheet of paper, leaving a margin on each side. Cut concentric circles from one large paper circle. Weave each circle through the V-shaped warp.

One solid yellow circle was torn out of paper and then torn into smaller and smaller open circles of different widths. Each open circle was then woven separately through a background of straight black warp.

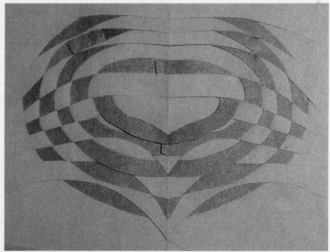

Front and back views of a circular shape woven into a warp of curved lines.

Directional Warp

Warps do not have to be strictly vertical. To make a slanted warp, mark a margin on all four sides of your paper, and then use a ruler to draw diagonal lines across it, starting at one corner and moving down the page.

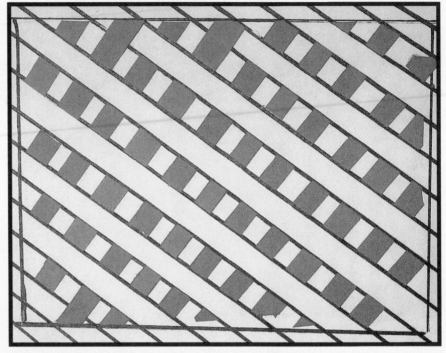

Strips of paper have been woven through this slanted warp.

In this weaving, the artist cut lines diagonally in different directions, and then wove paper strips through the irregular warp to form patterns.

Other Variations

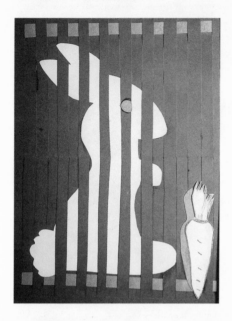

(left) **Shaped Weft** Weave a solid shape (in this case, a rabbit) over and under straight warp strips.

(right) **Shaped Weft** Shapes cut into shapes to form curves help create an imaginative weft.

Drawing with Weaving Slip a completed crayon drawing under a warp made with yarn.

Outlined Shape Weave a solid, dark shape (here it is a palm tree) in and out of white warp strips. Use black marker to accent shapes.

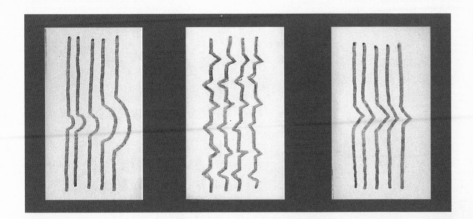

Optical Weaving First experiment with line possibilities, before cutting the warp.

Optical Weaving The artist wove straight black weft strips through this optically patterned warp.

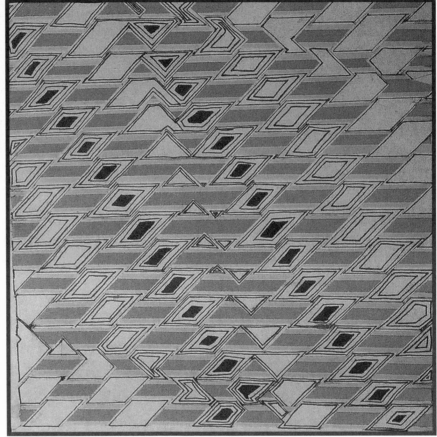

Optical Weaving Straight weft strips contrast with jagged warp to create an optical vibration. Pen and ink accents add to the effect.

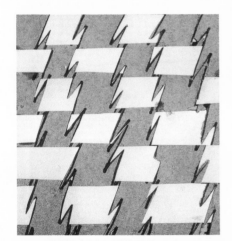

Optical Weaving Lines drawn in black marker give a jagged design even more drama.

3

Scrim

You can create imaginative patterns by weaving colorful threads into the fabric background of *scrim*, or rug canvas. (This is not to be confused with the translucent material used in stage sets, which is also called scrim.) Scrim has fairly large holes that allow you to push or pull thread and yarn easily through the mesh. You may change or rearrange the design by removing or placing the threads in new positions.

The stiffness of scrim gives the weaving body, making it easy to use without a frame and practical for any grade level. A first grader can easily learn the basic technique of over-and-under weaving; older students and adults can experiment with more intricate techniques.

In addition to its weaving possibilities, scrim can be used as a background for making hooked rugs. (For more on rug hooking, see Chapter 13.)

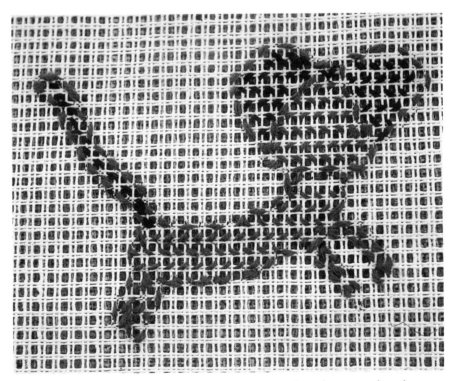

Young weavers should be encouraged to use yarn colors that appeal to them. Student work, grade 2.

(opposite) A simple portrait woven into scrim. Student work, grade 2.

PROCEDURE

There are two basic approaches to scrim weaving. You can let the shape emerge by weaving spontaneously into the scrim material. Alternatively, you can make a preplanned design.

To make a preplanned design, first draw the shape you would like to weave on a sheet of paper.

Place the scrim on top of the paper and use a crayon or felt-tip pen to trace over the design, thereby duplicating it.

Weave over and under the scrim fibers to outline the shape or, with the same weaving procedure, fill in solid areas.

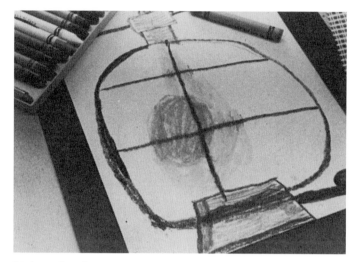

Make a drawing.

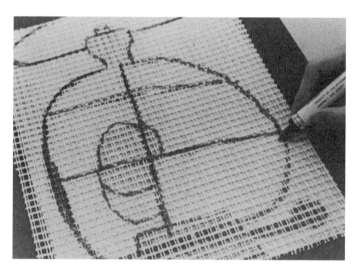

With the drawing beneath the scrim, trace over the drawing's main lines.

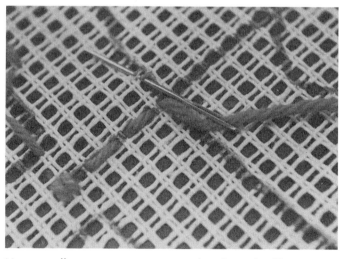

Use a needle to weave yarn over and under scrim fibers.

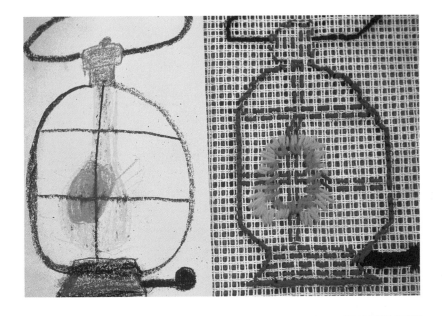

Combinations of short and long stitches add interest in this horse portrait. Student work, grade 2.

Drawings and weavings side by side.

VARIATIONS

Here are just a few additional ideas for working with scrim. Experimentation will lead you to discover many others.

- Cut out areas and make yarn span open spaces.
- Overlap yarns to create texture and line.
- Weave wire of various gauges, tree bark, or cellophane into the scrim.
- Cut shapes out of scrim to make mobile forms.
- Combine appliqué with weaving: Cut pieces of fabric and paste or stitch to the scrim.
- Superimpose scrim on other backgrounds such as wire mesh and burlap. Combine scrim weaving with rug hooking.

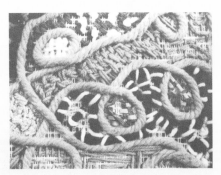

Stitching and gluing yarn onto scrim yields a densely textured, lively work.

4

WEAVING INTO
Cotton Mesh

BASIC MATERIALS
old picture frames or wood frames
cotton mesh netting
stapler
wool of various colors
needles
scissors

Optional Materials
pipe cleaners
raffia
ribbon
strings

Many types of cotton mesh provide weaving possibilities, and each offers exciting opportunities to experiment with threads and invent your own weaving method. The mesh serves as a background, allowing you to weave threads into it to form patterns. The design takes shape when you weave the yarn under and over the threads. As you complete each part of a shape, the design seems to spring to life.

Cotton mesh is available in curtains, mosquito netting, onion bags, and dishcloths. You can also purchase it by the yard. You'll want to experiment with different types of mesh to discover the potential of the material.

Collecting unusual materials to weave into the mesh can stimulate ideas for more provocative design possibilities. Try using natural materials such as grasses, dried flowers, or ferns. The luxurious colors and textures of synthetic yarn fibers are inspiring. Even pipe cleaners can be bent in, around, and through the mesh. As you and your students work, you'll become more alert to mesh materials and their potential for aesthetic expression.

Student work, grade 4.

(opposite) The visible mesh helps provide texture in this portrait.

29

PROCEDURES

Frames

Because mesh is a flimsy material, it works best when fastened to a frame.

Wood Frame   Use any wood frame, such as a picture frame, to hold the mesh. Cut the mesh a little larger than the opening and staple it to the frame.

Staple mesh securely to a wood frame.

Cardboard Frame   Use any heavy cardboard that will not bend when the mesh is stretched tightly over the frame opening. Pieces of corrugated boxes or foamcore are effective.

Approaches to Weaving

An exciting and challenging way of weaving is to work **spontaneously** with both material and design. This means weaving directly into the mesh without previous planning. Thread several needles, then experiment with colorful yarns and weaving patterns by changing or rearranging them, until a satisfying pattern emerges.

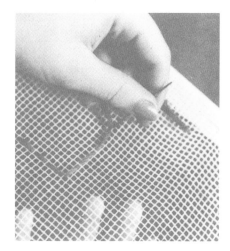

To work spontaneously, weave your yarn under and over the threads of the mesh to form a design.

(right) The finished weaving. Student work, grade 4.

Sometimes you might want a **planned design** of a single object. To begin, place your frame on a piece of paper and draw around the inside of the frame. Attach the mesh to the frame. Create a shape that will fit the size of the frame. Place the frame, with mesh face-down on the drawing so that the drawing appears through the mesh. With crayon or felt marker, draw over the lines of the drawing. The design now shows on the mesh. With a needle and thread, outline and fill in the design. Make some lines straight, some wavy or circular. This will add variety to the finished piece.

(left) Draw a shape that fits the proportions of your frame.

(below) With your drawing under the mesh, trace over the lines.

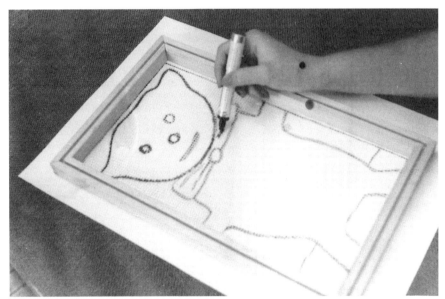

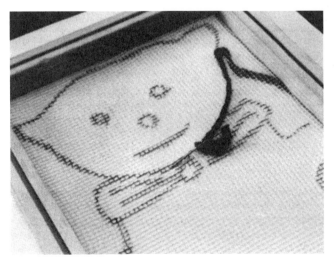

Work your threaded needle in and out of the mesh, following the drawing.

VARIATIONS

Here are some additional suggestions to explore.

- Use the background as part of the design, covering only parts of it with thread or yarn.
- Combine large, soft yarns with thin, harder ones.
- Use metallic, shiny materials with dull, smooth ones.
- Add knots, puffs, or loops to add dimension.
- Superimpose the woven mesh over another fabric or over paper.
- Cut a shape out of the mesh and superimpose it over burlap with pulled threads, then weave colorful yarns into the mesh and burlap.
- Stitch completed weavings together to make a wall hanging; mount on dowel rods.

Cutting a shape out of the mesh and mounting the weaving on colored paper creates an interesting positive/negative shape combination.

A strong black outline gives this bird clarity and visual strength.

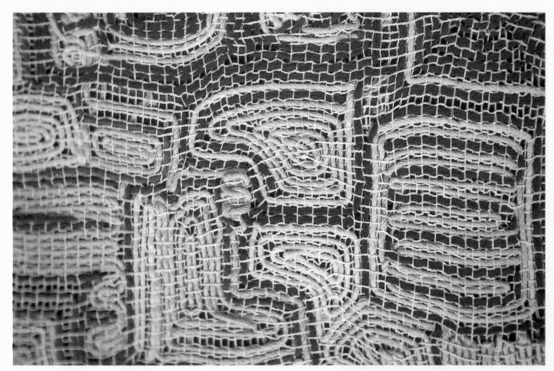

Abstract designs lend themselves to spontaneous weaving.

Enlarging the head of an animal allows the inclusion of smaller elements, such as whiskers and eye details.

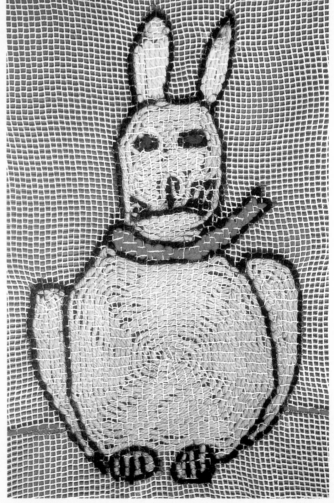

Notice how lines are emphasized by the direction of the weaving.

5

WEAVING INTO Burlap

BASIC MATERIALS
burlap
yarn
needles
scissors
straight pins
frame

Optional Materials
string
fabrics
cotton
felt
velvet
threads
reed

Burlap impresses children with its texture and color and is an ideal material for weaving as well as for drawn thread techniques. Like scrim and cotton mesh, burlap's threads are woven so loosely that other materials can easily be woven into them. While burlap can be purchased by the yard in many beautiful colors, the most practical background colors are natural, hemp, white, or eggshell. Burlap sacks for potatoes and grains also may be used for weaving if they are first washed, pressed, and cut into specific sizes.

First graders created weavings based on their initial drawings.

(opposite) Weave different sets or combinations, such as over-two and under-three threads, to form a pattern. Student work, grade 1.

35

DESIGNING ON BURLAP

To begin a design, weave colorful string, thread, or yarn in different sets or combinations, such as over-two and under-three burlap threads. This will form a pattern on the burlap. Weave many rows of one combination close together before starting another. Avoid leaving long strands of unwoven thread or yarn that appears as stitchery.

This student is using a large-eye needle to weave into burlap.

First graders created weavings based on their initial drawings.

The student wove over and under threads to form an outline, and then used stitchery techniques to create the decorative spots on the dog.

Pulled Thread Technique

When threads are pulled or rearranged, new compositions emerge. The pulled thread technique, though simple, can trigger unusual designs for wall hangings, draperies, room dividers, or window coverings. Start experimenting, and you may find new channels of thought opening up and new questions arising, such as: What will happen if I only pull weft threads? Could I rearrange threads to form ovals, curves, and angles? How can I use textures effectively to influence the design?

Discover and invent to achieve variety. Pull alternate strands to make a loose weave. Draw strands of threads and move parts of the remaining strands up or down to form curved lines, using your fingers to guide the position of the

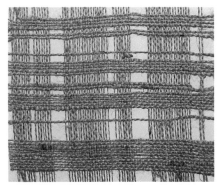

Create irregular spaces by pulling warp and weft threads at uneven intervals.

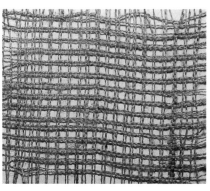

Pulling threads at regular intervals results in a repeated pattern.

threads. Pull a series of both warp and weft threads to create open spaces. Pull horizontal threads between sections of unpulled fabric to produce the effect of alternate strips.

Draw all the horizontal threads, leaving only a band of solid fabric to hold the warp intact. Then group the vertical threads together

into sections. Remove weft threads and tie the warp threads in groups to form spaces. Pull weft threads partially out, leaving open spaces and a fringe. Weave other threads into the fringe and open design. Weave ravelings into the burlap. The result is an unusual texture and color pattern.

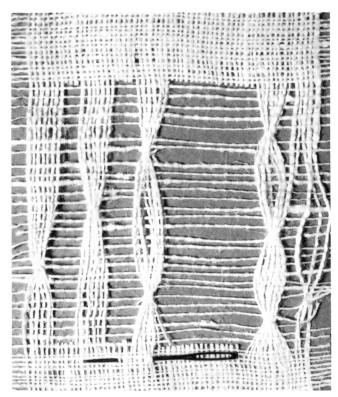

Pulling threads from the middle leaves a band of burlap at top and bottom. Tying some threads together creates interesting spaces.

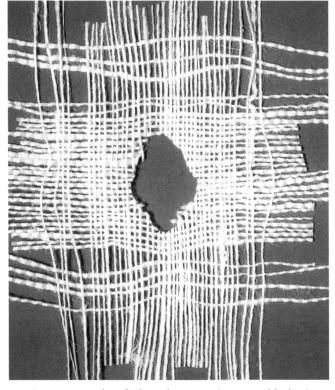

Cutting warp and weft threads, or cutting actual holes in the burlap, produces unusual effects.

Tying groups of threads with contrasting yarn adds movement and interest to this composition.

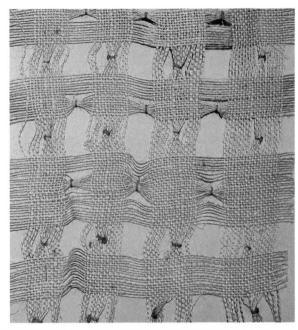

This artist pulled weft threads, tied them to create a repeated pattern, and added decorative stitches.

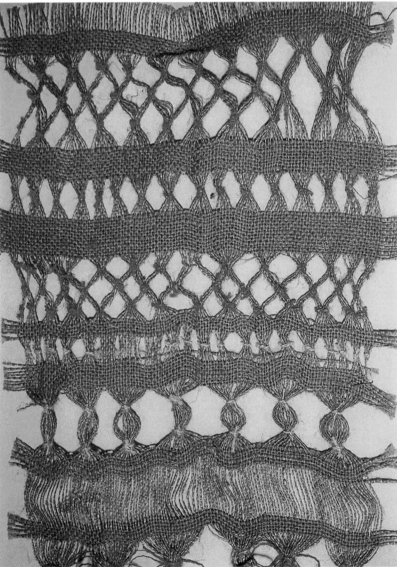

Warp threads are grouped to form varying spaces.

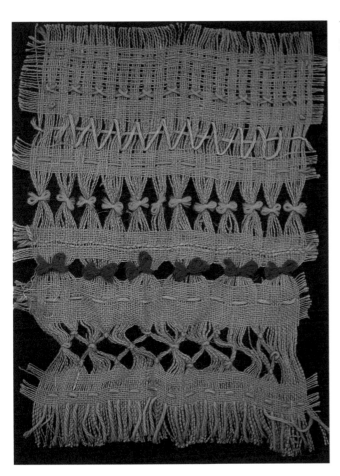

This artwork combines stitching, tying, and weaving. Vibrant yarn colors help make it lively.

Here, burlap ravelings of different colors have been woven into a contrasting burlap background. Leaving the ends exposed creates an internal fringe.

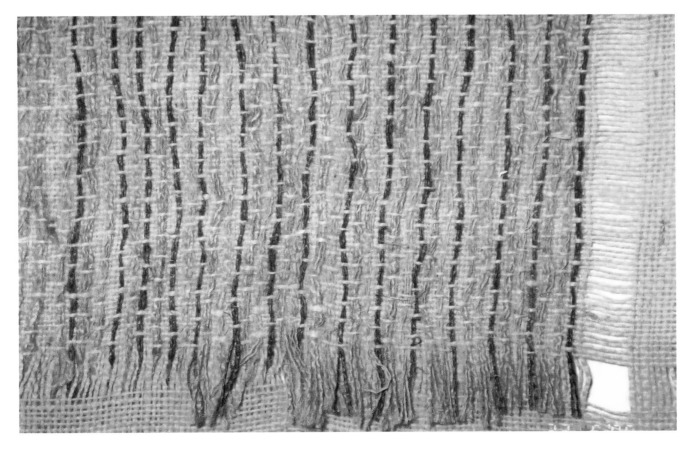

VARIATIONS

Burlap lends itself to mixed media experiments. The burlap surface will accept wet or dry drawing and printing media, and it complements the textures of other fabrics. Here are just a few ideas to get you started:

- Combine stitchery, appliqué, or rug hooking with burlap weaving.

- Superimpose nets or other loosely woven materials over the burlap weaving, and then add stitchery to tie the design together.
- Combine solid areas of burlap weaving with drawn work.
- Try a variety of printing methods: silk screen, block printing, eraser printing, monoprinting, or potato printing.

- Make a design with crayon on the burlap.
- Use stitchery and weaving to add emphasis.
- Weave colorful yarns through the open spaces resulting from drawn threads.

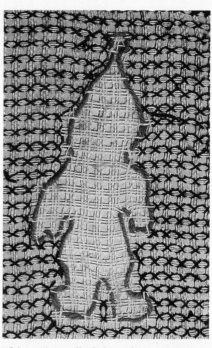

This artist pulled threads in a regular pattern, wove thinner yarn to form the outline, and added cross-stitches at nearly every point where warp and weft cross each other.

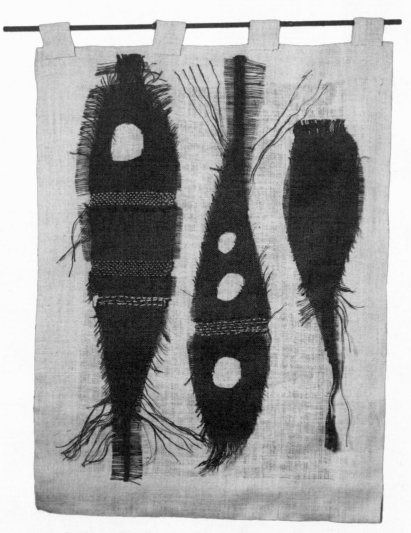

To make this pulled thread wall hanging, the author cut fish shapes from burlap, cut circles from the shapes, and wove into the fish shapes with yarn. The shapes are attached to a burlap background.

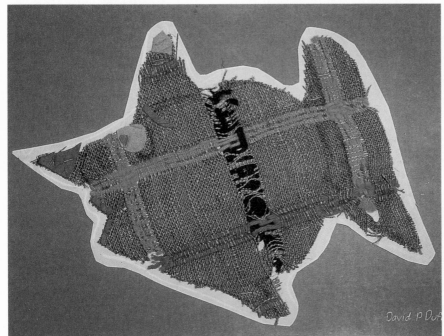

After weaving into this fish shape with yarn, the student used larger paper, cut to the same shape, as a contrasting border.

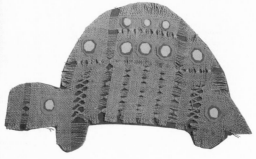

This turtle-shaped weaving has pulled thread and felt appliqué accents. The burlap has been adhered to cardboard to help hold its shape.

This weaving shows felt appliqué and pulled and tied thread techniques.

6

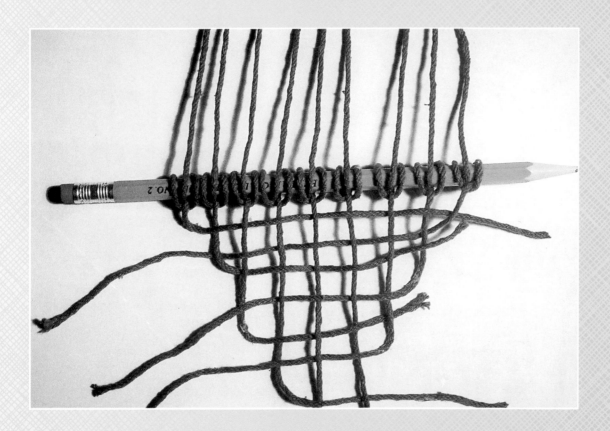

WEAVING ON A Pencil

BASIC MATERIALS

pencil, ruler, dowel, or broom handle
yarns of assorted colors and textures
(preferably heavy yarns)
scissors

Optional Materials
raffia
twine
plastic gimp
string
roving
ribbon
leather
nontoxic rubber cement or adhesive

PROCEDURE

To begin pencil weaving, first decide on the length of the form you want to make. Because the warp strands will be woven over and under one another, cut strands of yarn approximately one and a half times the length of your planned weaving. Loop the yarn so that it has one short tail of about six inches and one much longer tail, and follow the procedure shown in the photographs.

A weaving process need not be complicated or expensive to be successful and effective. Rich experiences in design are possible with common, inexpensive materials. A pencil can become the vehicle for a simple weaving process. Its use is related to the early looms, which consisted of nothing more elaborate than warp threads tied to a beam. To create pencil weavings you'll attach warp fibers to a pencil and use your fingers as tools. You can also use any rod-type object in place of the pencil—try a dowel or a broom handle and see what other ideas occur to you.

Loop the yarn so it has a short and long tail and place the pencil across the loop.

Fold the top part of the loop over the pencil.

Pull the short and long ends of the warp thread through the loop and pull tight. This holds the thread on the pencil by forming a knot.

Front and back views of properly looped warp threads.

43

The threads on each end of the pencil will later be used as the weft. To avoid confusion, these threads should be a different color than the warp threads. The six-inch tails can be put under a book or other heavy object to hold them and the pencil in place during the weaving.

Beginning at the left of the warp, weave the first end thread over and under all the way to the right. Then weave the end thread on the right back to the left. Weave the second thread on the left through to the right. Then bring the second thread at the right down and weave it back to the left. Use the third thread for weaving. When the weaving is completed, knot the ends in pairs. Remove the loops from the pencil and knot them in the same manner.

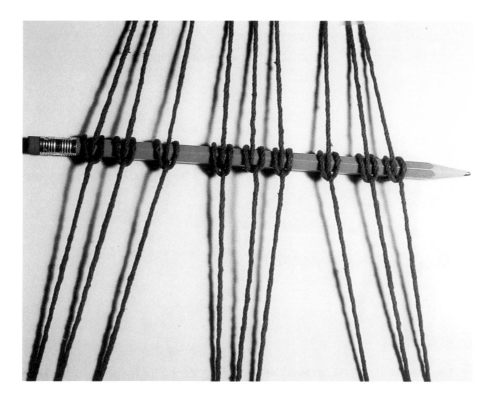

Loop as many threads as you like or that can fit across the length of your pencil.

Weave the left end thread over and under the warp all the way across, from left to right.

Weave the right end thread over and under from right to left.

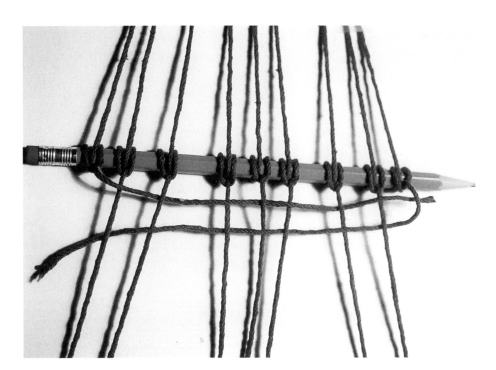

Weave the second from left thread over and under from left to right. Continue, alternating left and right threads until the weaving is complete.

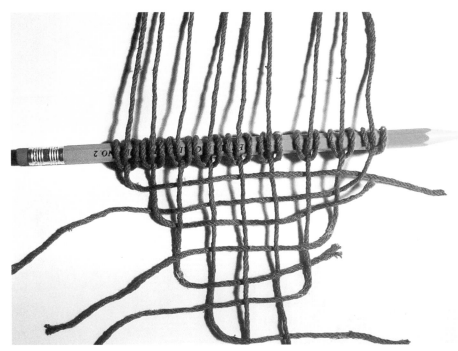

VARIATIONS

Slender forms are not the only possible results of pencil weaving. You can make wider forms by varying the number of warp strands and the length of the pencil or rod. Simple or intricate designs result when thin and thick yarns are used together; when tabby and tapestry techniques are combined in the same design; or when finished forms are stitched together to make a single shape.

Pencil weaving assumes another dimension when the pencil is attached to cardboard and the warp threads are stretched to produce a spider web design. Begin by tying the warp to the pencil, using the same basic procedure previously described. Cut slits on all edges of a piece of cardboard at reg-

ular intervals. Place the pencil slightly below the slits on the top edge. Anchor the short ends of the warp in the top slits and long strands at different positions in the side slits. By pulling the warp threads in different directions, you'll create a pattern similar to a spider web. Rearrange the threads in different slits to change the design.

To finish the weaving, remove the pencil, leaving the spider web pattern on the cardboard. The completed work is even more effective if the color of the original yarn design contrasts with that of the cardboard. It may also be placed in a mat or frame, or removed and superimposed on a fabric background.

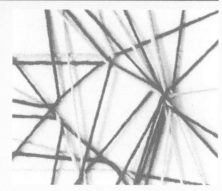

Examples of the spider web effect.

This warp is tied to a broom handle.

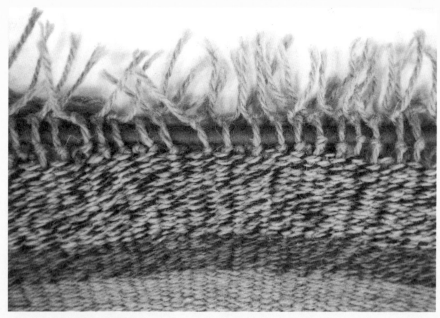

Detail of the finished piece on a broom handle.

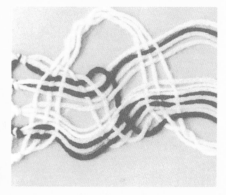

By weaving loosely and permitting spaces to develop between the intertwined threads, the final result will be a woven form.

Wonderful abstractions are possible with this technique.

7

BASIC MATERIALS

wire screen, screen mesh, window
screen, hardware cloth (large square
mesh), or chicken wire
yarn
strong wire cutters
scissors
needles
masking tape

Optional Materials

burlap	wools
straw	pipe cleaners
beads	tissue paper
ribbon	weeds
lace	felt
cellophane	raffia

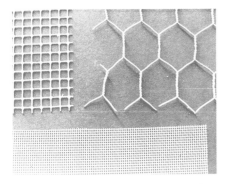

Types of wire mesh: hardware cloth
(left); chicken wire (right); screen
mesh (bottom).

Large-eye needles are best for weaving yarn through wire.

(opposite) The student used yarn
and fabric strips to make this simple
portrait. Courtesy Joan Foucht,
Columbus, Ohio.

Weaving a variety of types and strips of fabrics in wire mesh opens fresh
new avenues of creative expression. Because wire comes in various
meshes, you can choose the size of mesh that best serves your intent.
You can manipulate the wire into three-dimensional shapes, cut out
parts, or superimpose cutout areas over a screen of different mesh to
create a multidimensional effect.

Wire meshes of many types are available everywhere, and each has
possibilities and limitations as backgrounds for weaving. As you work,
be sensitive to color, texture, and pattern; consider their potential at
each point in design development, and integrate the wire and surface
enrichment to create a pleasing whole. The simple over-under process of
weaving into mesh can result in unusual and effective designs as you
experiment and explore with aesthetics in mind. Thus, you can express
your ideas in many different directions, using a variety of materials,
tools, and weaving patterns.

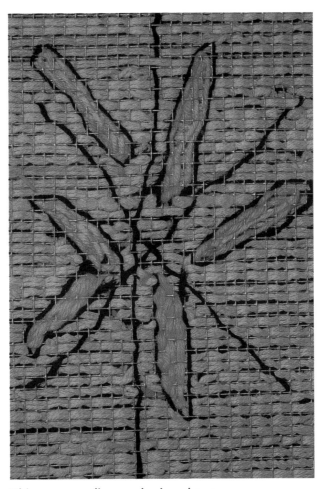

This woven outline emphasizes shape.

PROCEDURE

An inquiring mind is your best ally as you search for new ideas and ways of handling materials. Feel the screen mesh, yarn, string, and fabric. What ideas do these materials suggest for weaving? What can you do with wire mesh that is different from scrim or cotton mesh?

Spontaneous Weaving

Cut the wire and bind it with masking tape to prevent scratches. Begin to weave materials into the mesh background. As the weaving progresses, analyze its design qualities. View it from a distance, or, if you are making a sculptural form, at different angles. Does the design fit the space? Have you repeated colors and textures to make the design a pleasing unit? Are the weaving patterns that go over and under the wires varied enough to make a pleasing design?

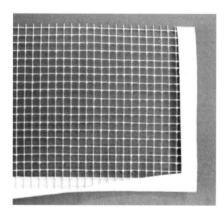

Binding wire edges with masking tape will prevent you from being scratched as you weave.

Preplanned Designs

Planning your design beforehand is another way to begin a weaving. Here is one possible procedure: Place the wire frame on a piece of paper and draw around it. With a crayon, draw a design on the paper. Place the wire mesh over the design. With a felt marker, trace the design to duplicate it on the wire.

Draw around your wire form to establish the outer edges of a planned design.

Draw your design.

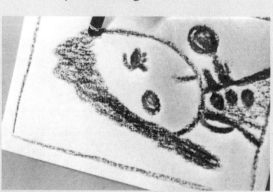

With your drawing under the wire, trace over it with a felt-tip marker.

Use your weaving medium—yarn, string, fabric—to cover drawn areas of the design.

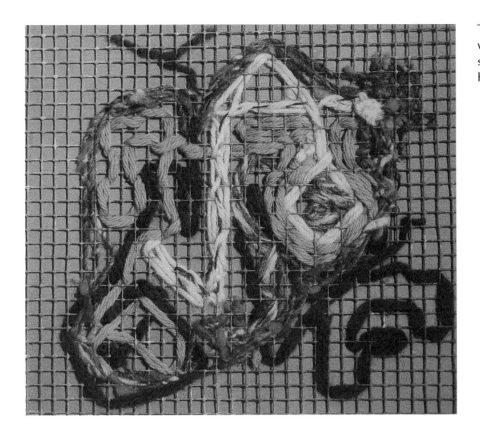

Try weaving with yarn of varying weights or with yarns containing slubs. The wire shown here is called hardware cloth.

Pattern and Texture

Using single strands of yarn creates one type of pattern, while double or triple strands result in still other designs. You can achieve interesting surface treatments by using a variety of materials—weeds, unique threads, and different types of yarn. Leaving areas of wire exposed will vary the pattern and add to the overall design.

Accent

Wool or cotton yarns often need other materials for accent. Raffia may be woven into the mesh to add colorful and textural patterns. Roving, a coarse cotton fiber, can also give dramatic textural quality.

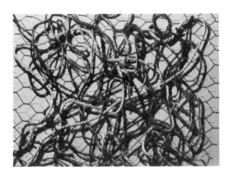

Even ordinary twine can be incorporated successfully into wire weavings. This weaving is done on chicken wire.

Using the wire grid as a basis for your design can yield appealing abstract patterns.

VARIATIONS

The possibilities inherent in this technique are limited only by imagination, and range from simple, expressive forms made by children to room dividers, wall hangings, and sculptural forms reflecting the experience and skill of professional adults.

You might begin your experiments with chicken wire, which is one of the most common wire meshes. Chicken wire is highly useful as a background if you want to tie or weave fibers around the wire to span or connect areas of yarn.

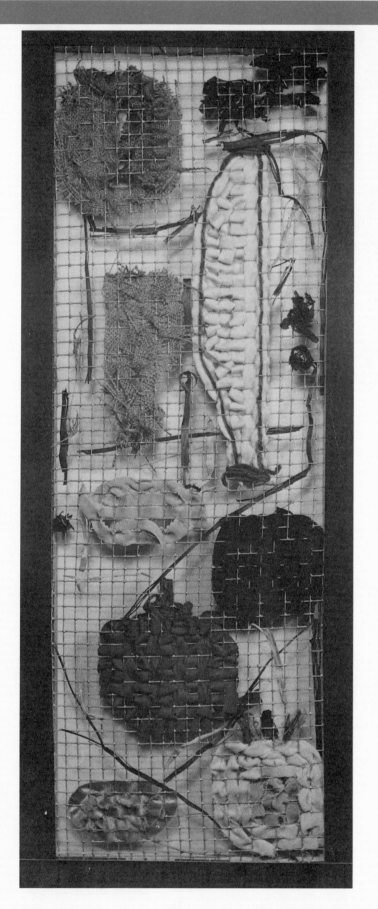

Fabric, raffia, and burlap woven into hardware cloth. Student work, grade 3.

A mixture of yarn weights and textures give this composition on hardware cloth a three-dimensional appearance.

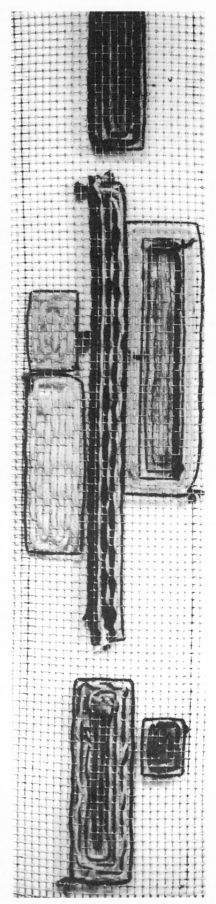

Window screen, a fine mesh, encourages the use of threads and finely textured yarns. Hardware cloth calls for thick yarns and bulky fabrics. Any of these types of wire mesh can be accented with gold or bronze spray paint. Weaving and fabric appliqué can also be combined when designing in mesh.

The artist wove a variety of yarns into window screen. Student work, grade 6.

8

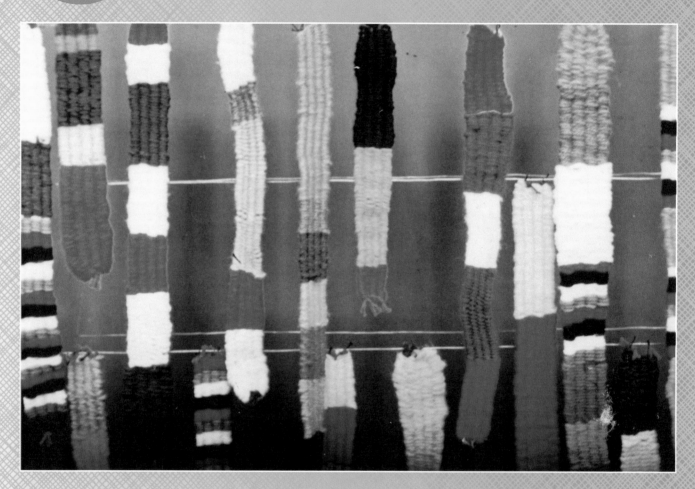

WEAVING WITH Straws

BASIC MATERIALS
straws (thick or thin, paper or plastic)
scissors
string
yarn

Optional Materials
thick and thin yarns
tinsel
fabric cut into strips
ribbon
nylon stockings cut into strips
cords

The everyday drinking straw offers weavers an opportunity to become acquainted with yet another process that requires no mechanical loom. In this technique, straws become the framework that holds the warp. The larger the diameter of the straw, the easier it is to push or pull yarn or string through it. Narrow or wide forms, made by using varied numbers of straws, can be woven into colorful belts, ingenious ties, and striking wall hangings.

Weaving with soda straws, which are larger in diameter than regular drinking straws.

(opposite) A colorful display of straw weavings.

PROCEDURE

Cut drinking straws in half and cut one warp string for each straw. Strings should be equal in length and as long as the finished product will be. Tie all the warp strings together in a knot. Place the knotted end of warp at the top of the straws, and then thread each string through a separate straw. Suck on the straw to get the string through easily.

Push the straws up to the knotted ends. See [A] opposite.

Weave over and under the straws, beginning a pattern. See [B] and [C].

Add a new color by tying a knot to the previous color and continue the weaving. As the weaving progresses, push the woven sections up and off the straws to free them for more weaving. (See example this page.)

Slip the straws off the warp when the weaving is finished. Weave the end strings into one another so they will not ravel.

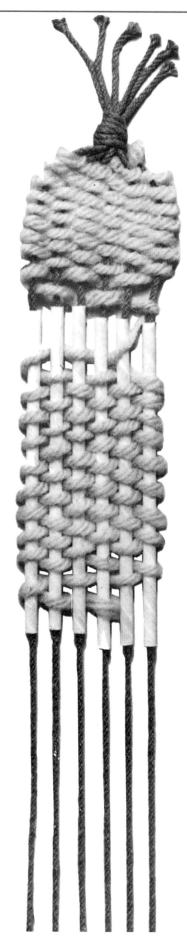

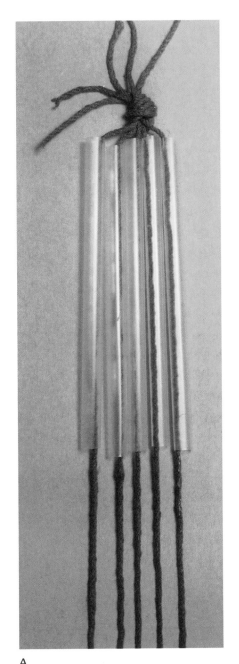

A

B

C

VARIATIONS

Use several strands of warp through each straw to provide additional warp threads for more intricate weaving. To vary the materials used for weft, try using some of the optional materials listed at the beginning of this chapter. Use pieces of straw as part of the finished design. Sew completed pieces into new forms, or superimpose them on a burlap background.

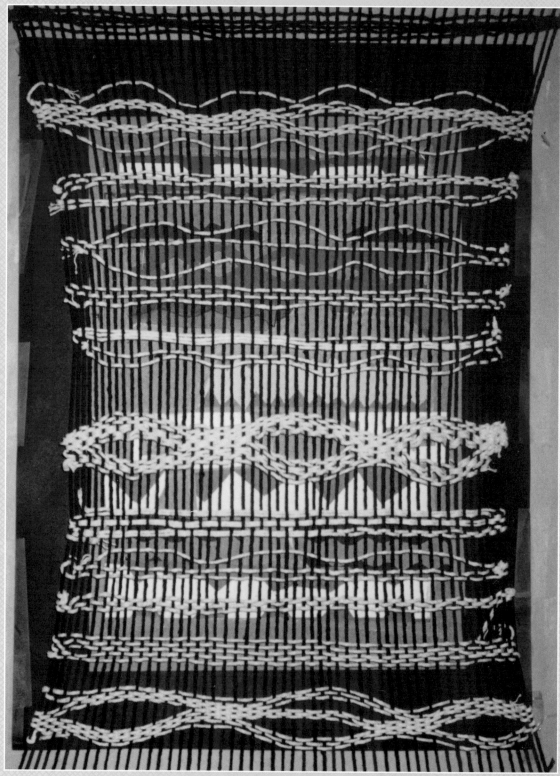

9

WEAVING ON Cardboard

BASIC MATERIALS
heavy cardboard
string
yarn
scissors
ruler

Optional Materials
ribbon
raffia
crepe paper
tissue paper

Using a piece of cardboard to stretch warp is traditional, yet its practicability and economy still intrigue the experimental weaver. There are many advantages inherent in this form of weaving. You can cut the cardboard into various shapes and sizes. You can easily rearrange the warp and weft as you experiment. The cardboard can remain as backing for the completed weaving, or the weaving can be removed from the cardboard and displayed as a woven form. Several pieces of cardboard weaving can be stitched together to make a wall hanging, afghan, or rug. Finally, experimental pieces woven on cardboard can serve as a base for planning larger weavings. The cardboard technique, plus a little imagination, opens exciting new avenues of expression.

As you design your weaving, don't limit yourself to row after row of color in a tabby weave. You'll want to expand your thinking to include the emotional impact of cool, warm, vivid, or somber colors. Consider the relationship of color and texture, the possibilities of textural combinations, and the effects to be gained from using varied weaving techniques. Dealing with tactile materials encourages expression through texture.

This necklace, made on cardboard, includes reed sticks woven into the yarn to give structure and help hold the necklace flat. Warp strands are knotted at the bottom to create a fringe. By author.

[opposite] Beneath this black and white cardboard weaving is a colored paper-and-crayon composition that adds complexity to the work.

Grouping warp threads or weaving some parts of the warp more tightly than others will result in different patterns.

PROCEDURE

Warp Threads

The warp threads running from top to bottom of the cardboard provide the structural skeleton for the weaving operation. The warp may be superimposed on cardboard and anchored in slits, or held in position by a cardboard frame. The arrangement of the structural skeleton definitely influences the final design. Any rearrangement of the warp changes the ultimate pattern of the piece being woven.

One method of placing warp on cardboard does not require a frame. To use this method, draw a line along the top and bottom of the cardboard about a half inch from the edge. Cut slits from the edge to this line, about a half inch apart. Anchor the warp in the top slits, and stretch the fibers to the bottom of the cardboard.

A second method is to attach the warp to a cardboard frame. This permits working from both front and back of the weaving. Cut four strips of cardboard. Make slits in the two pieces used for top and bottom of the frame, making sure that there are an equal number of slits on each side. Next, staple the four pieces of cardboard together, pointing slits outward so that they serve as serrations through which the warp can be looped. Pull the warp just tight enough so that it will lie flat on the frame.

The simplest way to arrange the warp is to space the threads at equal intervals. However, placing the warp strands at unequal distances from one another lends variety and interest, and allows you to experiment and discover new and

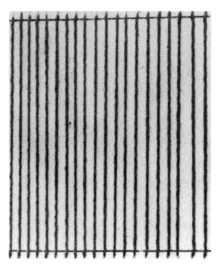

A straight yarn warp, stretched from top slits to bottom.

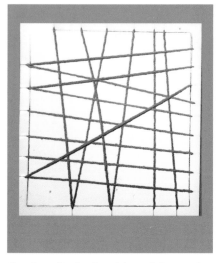

Cutting slits in the sides of the cardboard, as well as the top and bottom, creates interesting effects in the final weaving.

Weft threads swirl through the warp in a silhouette-like pattern.

varied weaves. Still another kind of pattern, and a more intricate method, makes use of cut slits in the sides as well as the top and bottom of the cardboard.

Weft

Horizontal threads (the weft) add bulk to the structural skeleton as they are woven over and under the warp. By combining different weaves or techniques and an inventive use of weft you can create unusual and attractive patterns.

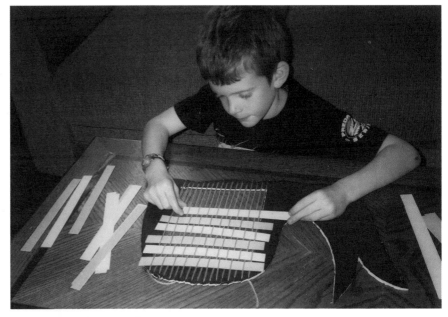

Strips of paper, tagboard, or fabric can serve as weft. *Whaleweave*, by Sean Madden, age 7.

This cardboard weaving was made using tapestry techniques (see page 85). Student work by Ryan Kidd, grade 3. Courtesy of Eileen Scally.

Several cardboard weavings were sewn together to create this wall hanging.

The warp was woven several times through each slit. Then pale weft threads were woven through the warp to create the design.

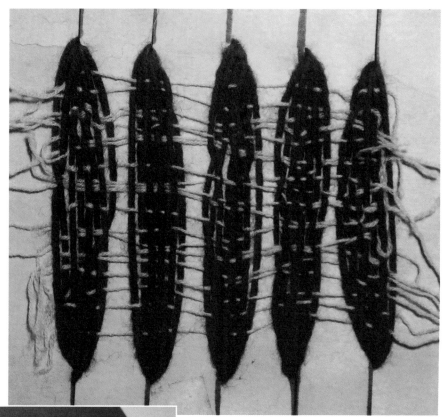

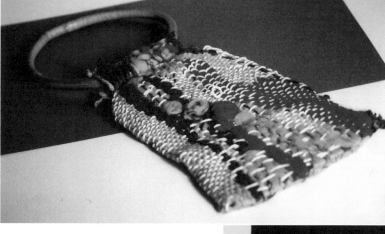

To make this purse, the artist wrapped warp threads and wove weft threads around both sides of a cardboard form. The top edge of the weaving was left open so that the form could be slipped off the cardboard. Courtesy Patricia Palmieri.

The warp threads were wrapped around the cardboard form (left). Horizontal threads were woven around both sides of the cardboard form. The result is a pocket effect or purse. Courtesy Eileen M. Seally.

VARIATIONS

Frame

Cut slits in the edges of the cover of a shoe box or gift box. Anchor the warp in the slits, then stretch it across the box top. The result is a shadow-box effect with the design varying according to the depth of lid and slits. Use a variety of cardboard shapes to obtain interesting forms. A collar-shaped cardboard, for example, is a useful base for weaving yarns and beads into collars and jeweled necklines.

Box top with yarn pulled through slits on all four sides. Student work, college.

To create this weaving, a circle of cardboard was slit around the edges; a hole was placed in the center. The warp was anchored in the slits and wrapped around both sides of the circle.

This circular weaving, made of string, is mounted on white fabric.

The cardboard shape can become part of the final design, with weaving used as an accent.

Warp

Use different warp arrangements, or tie some of the warp strings together, leaving open spaces. Weave other areas solid.

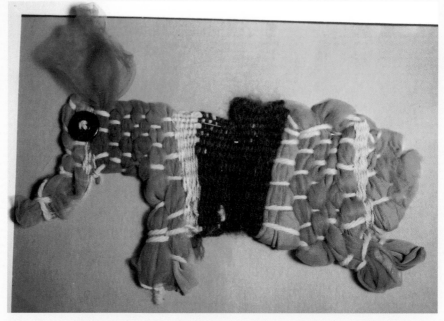

Cut your cardboard in a particular shape and the final weaving will reflect it.

Woven form with exposed warp threads. Student work, college.

A magazine cover was pasted to cardboard. Slits made at top and bottom of the cardboard held the warp. The weaving was made over the cover, using the tapestry technique so that the image appeared to be part of the total design.

Weft

Experiment with different loop techniques. Try weaving yarn of contrasting color between two warp strands, carrying it in back of the tabby weaving and over the front to form a loop. Or begin with a tabby weave (over and under the alternate warp threads). Form loops by lifting the weft of alternate warp threads and inserting a rod, stick, or brush handle. Weaving several more rows of tabby will hold the loops in place when the rod is removed.

Experiment with unusual weft materials. Try combining tissue paper, wool, and string. Use strips of synthetic leathers or cords, or reeds, dried grasses, or other materials from nature.

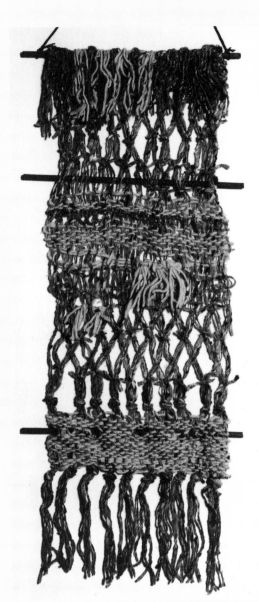

Dowel rods help hold the shape of, and give weight to, this cardboard weaving.

Tissue paper combined with yarn serves as weft material. Student work, college.

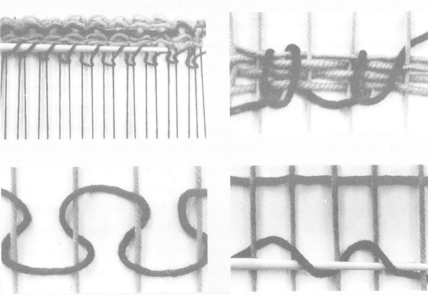

A variety of loop techniques.

10

WEAVING ON A Frame

BASIC MATERIALS
strips of wood
hammer
nails
string
yarn

Optional Materials
a discarded wood frame
fishing line
reed
nylon
weeds

Frames have been used for centuries when a more precise form of weaving was desired. Primitive weavers used many devices to weave the cloth they needed. The Peruvian frame on page 3 is one example.

Frames suitable for weaving can be cardboard, as suggested in Chapter 9, or made from strips of wood. They can be picture frames made of soft wood, stretcher frames used for oil painting, or simple handmade frames. They can be commercially designed specifically for weaving; or, on the other hand, they can be such ingenious devices as beach chairs turned upside-down.

(opposite) Found wood used as a frame. Cassandra Lee Tellier, *Untitled*. Wool and synthetic fibers, 19 x 25" (48 x 64 cm). Courtesy of the artist.

The frame—metal, in this case—can serve as part of the composition. Danish weaving, collection of the author.

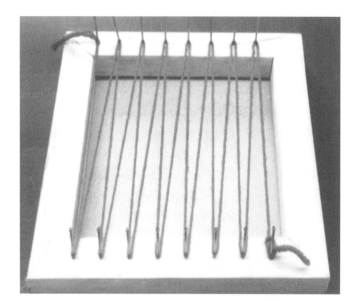

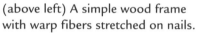

(above left) A simple wood frame with warp fibers stretched on nails.

(above right) A commercially-designed frame warped and woven with jute. Courtesy Lily Mills, Shelby, North Carolina.

Even a beach chair can serve as a wood frame. Courtesy Pearl Greenberg, Downtown Community School. Photo: Murray Greenberg.

PROCEDURE

Weaving on frames has several significant advantages, among which are their availability and versatility. Frames need not be standard squares or rectangles but may be made in different shapes.

To make a handmade frame, cut two equal lengths of softwood for the top and bottom of the frame and two longer pieces for the sides. Brads or corrugated fasteners hammered in at the corners will hold the frame together. Drive small nails at equal intervals along the top and bottom strips. Tie the warp to the first nail at the top, pull it down and around the first nail at the bottom, and up again to the next top nail, stretching the warp top to bottom until all the nails are used. Once you've stretched the warp, you're ready to weave.

Nails, equally or unequally spaced and arranged into patterns, lay a precise groundwork for the final weaving. Different kinds of carpet tacks and staples can be used. The frame may be more than a device for weaving, since you can consider using it as an integral part of the weaving design.

After deciding on the type and shape of the frame, decide on the specific material you'll use for weaving. Examine threads and yarns for color and texture. Innovate, experiment, and explore a vast range of materials, from the traditional to the new synthetics.

Avoid monotonous strips of color and tabby weave; instead, use imaginative approaches to design and technique. Explore textural combinations to add variety to your designs, using materials such as yarn, straw, nylon stockings, and weeds. Try different pattern formations: weave over two threads and under one; be creative with color combinations, using one color with another or interlocking color as in the tapestry technique. Experiment with special relationships, such as combining open areas with solidly woven areas.

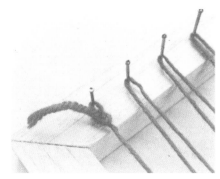

Stretch the warp from top to bottom of the frame until all the nails are used.

Vary the position of the nails to create different warp patterns.

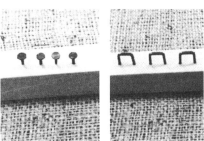

Carpet tacks and staples are suitable to hold warp threads for wood frame weaving.

This weaving was removed from its frame and used as a cushion top.

VARIATIONS

There are many ways to experiment when using a frame.

- Using the warp as part of the design, weave one section at a time. Make one section a tight weave; weave the other sections more loosely.

- Let the warp alone be the design for the center, creating an airy effect.
- Insert dowel rods to raise and lower the warp strands under different sets of fibers.
- Experiment with tapestry variations.
- Explore triangular or hexagonal frames.

- Make a frame in separate sections fitted together for large, unusual shapes.
- Use an orange crate as a frame. Place nails at each end, notch the wood, and loop the yarn around the notches.

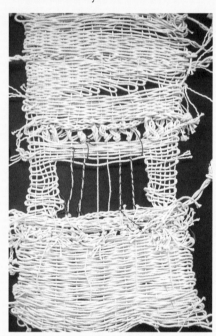

This weaver made a design using string woven on an orange crate. Student work, grade 3.

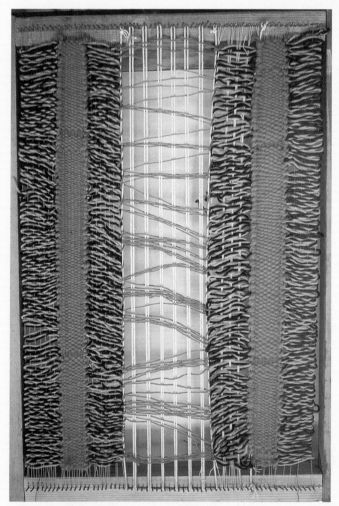

Alternating tightly woven areas with open ones provides visual interest in this weaving. Student work, college.

A drawer or box works well as a structure to hold the warp. The artist used dowel rods to raise the warp. Student work, college.

Chunky wools and thinner wools alternate with wide plastic and fabric strips in this weaving in progress. Student work, grade 6.

(above, top) Triangular frames offer many creative possibilities.

(above, bottom) Sections woven on several frames were fitted together to form this shape. Student work, college level.

Strips of burlap and yarn have been woven through these warp strings.

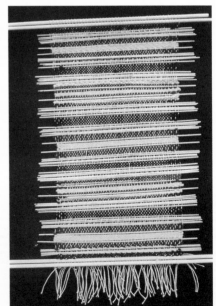

Many thin dowel rods woven through the warp give this weaving regularity and strength.

MOUNTING

Your weaving is truly complete when it has been mounted attractively. Wood frame weavings can be successfully removed from their frames and transferred to dowel rods. The weight of the dowels causes the finished piece to hang straight and remain flat.

To transfer a weaving from a frame to dowel rods, carefully remove the warp from the nails at one end and gently push the dowel through the series of loops that remain. Then remove the warp at the other end and place a dowel through those loops. If more weight is needed, purchase some small metal weights from a sewing shop or hardware store. Attach the weights at the bottom end of the back of the weaving, then cover them with a strip of fabric to give the weaving a neat appearance.

Weavings may remain mounted on the original work frame. You might also consider attaching molding to the front of the wood frame. This will cover the warp threads that suspend the weaving from the wood frame. You can also place your weaving in a picture frame or on mat board.

Gently slip the warp threads off the nails that held them and slip a dowel through the loops.

Weavings make beautiful pillows. Student work, college.

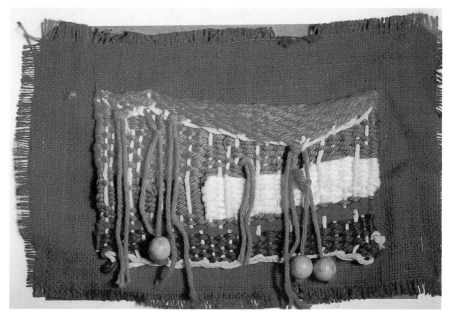

This weaving has been removed from its frame and mounted on burlap. Student work, grade 3.

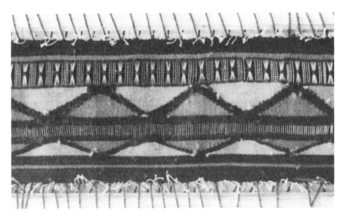

The warp was wrapped around 300 finishing nails to form this design.

This artist used fishing line for warp and fringe. Student work, college.

This weaving was made on a rectangular frame with binder's twine and strips of leather. Removed from the frame, it was folded in half and sewn to form a purse. Courtesy Gale Youngworth.

11

WEAVING WITH Reed

BASIC MATERIALS

sponge—to dampen reed and absorb
   excess water
pan for water—to soak reed
pincers or pliers—to hold or bend reed
scissors
ruler or tape measure
pencil—to mark measurements
sandpaper—to smooth rough areas
   when finished and dry
pen knife
round and flat reed

OPTIONAL MATERIALS

rattan
raffia
cords
strings and twines

Natural Materials

twigs
vines
grasses
pine needles
corn husks
cattails
mosses
stems
leaves
bark

Papers

crepe paper
tissue paper
cellophane

Materials Used by American Indians

white oak
river reed

Reed offers another dimension to the possibilities of weaving without a loom. While commonly used for contemporary items such as placemats, room dividers, door mats, purses, decorative animals, and the ubiquitous basket, reed weaving has not been developed fully as an art form. Reed's potential should challenge you to seek new ways to transform reed into imaginative baskets, exciting two- and three-dimensional woven shapes, wall hangings, and sculptural forms.

In the school curriculum, the use of reed is often limited to the making of traditional and often unremarkable baskets. However, the basic basketry process, one of the oldest methods of weaving, should not be disregarded by the contemporary reed weaver. Basketry techniques of weaving and decorating can be applied to experimental reed weaving. What begins as a traditional basket may emerge as a striking shape or

Sea grass basket being woven by Mary Jackson. © Karen Kasmauski/Corbis

(opposite) Traditional basket, Eritrea, Africa. © Frances Linzee Gordon/Getty Images

75

mobile. Even the decorative materials used in early basketry—stones, shells, teeth, feathers, porcupine quills—can inspire the designer-weaver of today. Natural dyes from seeds, fruits, and roots, and many other sources add interest and color.

More than one hundred years ago in his book *Indian Basketry*, Otis Mason said that the basket maker "must be botanist, colourist, weaver, designer, and poet, all in one." This is still true of the weaver of reed. Like a botanist, you must explore your surroundings in search of materials; like a colorist, you must know which plants, seeds, and juices make dramatic natural dyes; like any weaver, you must experiment with variation and repetition of weave; like a designer, you must assemble and develop forms and patterns that enhance each other; and like a poet, you must synthesize the parts into an aesthetic whole.

From the collection of Harold Krevolen.

Papago coil basket, Arizona. © Danny Lehman/Corbis

PROCEDURE

While natural plant reed is exciting as weaving material, commercial reed is usually more easily available and can be purchased in round or flat strands of various diameters and widths. Commercial reed often comes in skeins and is usually dry and brittle, but soaking it in water for a short time will make it pliable enough to be cut and manipulated. To make handles or spokes, cut the reed in specific lengths before soaking. Before soaking reed, roll it into a loose coil and fasten its end by twisting it into the coil. Because reed is most pliable while damp, wrap it in soft material such as terry cloth to keep it moist until needed.

It is helpful to know some basketry techniques when experimenting with reed weaving. First of all, a tight, firm base is essential to the entire form. The reeds of the base, called **spokes**, lie flat. Some spokes are inserted through slits of other spokes and all radiate from the center. You can cut them to the length you need for the base size or leave them long enough for weaving the entire form.

Round Base

Using soaked and pliable reed, select four spokes and cut a slit lengthwise in the middle of each. Make these slits large enough so that four additional spokes can be pushed through them. Lay the four spokes closely side by side. Place the four additional spokes, also close together, perpendicular to the first four and push them through the slits in the first four to form a symmetrical cross. The weaving proceeds around the center of this four-armed cross.

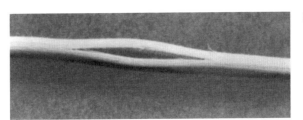

Split the reed lengthwise.

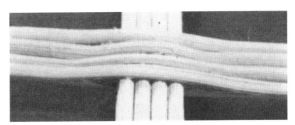

Push spokes through the slits.

To begin the weaving, use a thinner reed than that used for spokes. Bend it at its midpoint to form a loop around one of the four arms of the cross. Fit the reed close to the center of the cross and keep its two loose ends of equal length. Cross these ends and weave them around the second arm of the crosses. Cross the ends again and weave them around the third arm. Repeat with the fourth arm and continue to weave the two reed ends around the center of the cross. This is known as the **pairing technique.**

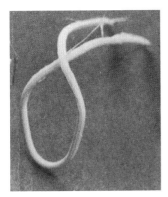

Bend thin reed to form a loop.

Cross ends and bend the loop around the arms of the cross.

Continue to cross and weave.

The next step is to separate the spokes of the cross, making them pairs of adjacent reeds. Weave reed-ends over and under these pairs often enough to hold the spokes firmly in place. Once more, separate the cross arms, this time making single spokes. Weave in and around each individual spoke until the base attains the desired circular shape and size. Using larger reed around the edge will strengthen the base.

You can make a variation of the simple round base by weaving a finish around the edge of the base, continuing to use the same pairing weave. First, decide on the diameter of the base, and then cut the base spokes at least six inches longer than the diameter. Continue weaving the base as previously described, using the pairing weave for the largest part of the base. When the base is the desired size, weave the extra lengths of the spokes into one another to form a finished edge.

Separate spokes into pairs and continue to weave around them.

Separate pairs of spokes into singles and continue weaving.

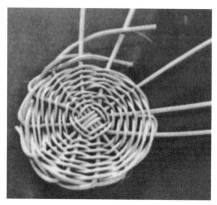

Weave the extra lengths of spokes into one another to form a decorative edge.

The finished base.

Oval Base

The oval base is a variation of the round base. Decide on the number of base spokes, then cut half of them to one length and the other half slightly shorter. Cut slits in the centers of the shorter group of spokes. Push the long spokes through these center slits. Space the short spokes some distance apart. Begin weaving with the pairing technique as explained previously. Continue to twist the thin reed around all the side or shorter spokes, then again around the whole group of spokes, and so on for at least two cycles.

Separate the groups of spokes into individual spokes as the weaving proceeds. Continue to pair-weave, pulling the spokes a little farther apart with each row of weaving to produce an oval shape. The pairing technique can then be used to finish off the edges.

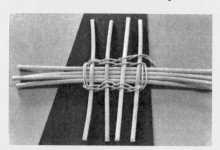

Form an oval base with one set of spokes close together, the other farther apart.

Twist thin reed around the spokes for at least two cycles.

Gradually separate the spokes as you weave.

Wooden Base

A wooden base can be any shape or size. Commercial bases usually come with holes drilled for the reed. However, you can cut your own wood base and drill holes to the size needed for the reeds.

Decide on the length of reed you need for constructing the sides. When the reed stands in a vertical position, it is called a **stake**. The basic stakes are those that fit into the holes and stand perpendicular to the base. Around these, the shape is woven.

To vary the design and give the ends that stick through the bottom a finished appearance, extend the stakes a few inches on the underside. Bend one stake-end down, weaving in and out around the

following three stakes. Continue this process until all stake-ends are woven in front and back of one another on the underside. Clip off the excess reed.

For variety, extend the basic stakes through the wood bottom and drive wooden beads onto the

Finish the bottom of a wooden base by weaving excess spoke lengths together.

Beads provide an attractive finish for a base.

reed. This not only holds the reed securely, but also produces an interesting base. If the beads are loose, because their holes are larger than the reeds, cut additional pieces of reed and stuff them into each bead hole. This will hold the beads in place.

Sides

The sides of the basket are an integral part of the base and rise from it. There are many ways of weaving the sides. After becoming familiar with one method, experiment with others.

Begin by bending the ends of the base reeds slightly upward. If the original base spokes are too stiff for easy bending, cut them off close to the woven base and insert more pliable reed between the original

base spokes. Another method is to insert vertical stakes through the spaces in the woven edging. These verticals provide a structure through which the form is woven. It is important to remember that unless the spokes are damp, they will not bend and may break.

The next step involves a fairly easy type of weaving called waling. **Waling** is used to strengthen the

form as its sides take shape. To do waling weave, use three strands of reed. Place two strands on opposite sides of a vertical stake; cross them and then pass them around the next stake. The third strand is then twined into the previous weave by weaving it over the top of the two crossed strands, then in front of the next two stakes and under the next cross.

Waling weave.

Waling combined with open work.

VARIATIONS

Side Variations

To achieve interest in spacing and accenting designs, use leather strips, wooden balls, bamboo bits, or beads as decorations. Combine round and flat reed. Vary the size of the round reed and the width of the flat reed. Insert extra stakes. Place round reed next to flat reed and alternate.

Wooden balls and beads work well as basket decorations.

Combine round and flat reed in the same basket.

Combine thin and thick stakes and wide and narrow reed.

Insert extra stakes in the lower part of the basket to vary the texture.

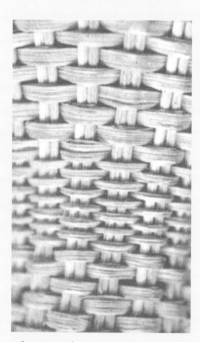

Alternate the use of round and flat reed.

Edges

Whatever form you create, the final edge gives it a finished appearance. Experiment to develop interesting and unusual edges. Try large loops, or bend the reed at unusual angles.

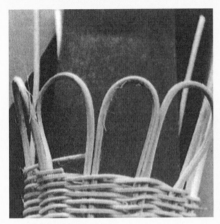

Large loops create an interesting edge treatment.

End stakes can be woven and tucked into the finished basket.

Bend stakes at an angle and allow them to overlap each other.

This seven-storey basket replica is the Newark, Ohio headquarters of the Longaberger Company. Longaberger baskets are handmade from thin strips of maple wood. The bottoms are woven first, then shaped over a mold. A thin band of wood is tacked on to finish the top.

NATIVE AMERICAN BASKETRY

Although basketry is highly commercialized today, some Cherokee Indians still practice the ancient weaving process of basketry as an art form. These weavers have retained their traditional techniques and use native materials. They work in a relaxed way, carefully planning and shaping each piece. A medium-sized basket may require three days to complete.

The photos on the facing page illustrate the Cherokee basket weaving process.

Photos courtesy Cherokee Historical Association, Inc., Cherokee, North Carolina.

Mohawk baskets. Collection of the author.

Cherokee basket. Collection of the author.

Basket materials prepared for weaving.

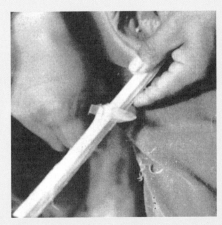

Removing rough areas from white oak.

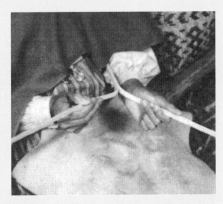

Separating white oak into strips.

Thinning the strips further.

Starting a basket.

Tightening the reed by pushing down on the horizontal reed bands.

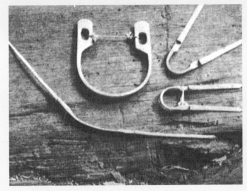

Various carved handles prepared for weaving.

Weaving with river cane.

A completed Cherokee basket. All photos this page by author, courtesy Cherokee Historical Association, Inc.

12

TAPESTRY Weaving

BASIC MATERIALS

cardboard or wood frame
string of assorted colors
wool
scissors
straight pins
weft materials:
    tinsel
    ribbon
    fabric
    yarn
    nylon stockings
    tissue paper
    cellophane
dowels, small strips of wood or
    cardboard

Optional Materials

assortment of weft supplies:
    leather
    reed
    jute
    rope
    glass and metal rods
    sticks or thin tree branches

This is the tapestry technique of interlocking threads and slits.

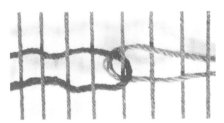

Another tapestry technique is to weave two weft threads around the same warp thread.

(opposite) Guatemalan tapestry weaver. © Topham/The Image Works

The word *tapestry* awakens visions of splendor and ingeniously woven scenes from a half-forgotten time when medieval artists immortalized with threads their legends, history, and everyday pursuits. Tapestries, particularly in the Middle Ages, were used in parades, at tournaments, and to adorn the walls of cathedrals and castles. Although an old art, the use of tapestry techniques today can add new interest to simple weaving patterns. There are many adaptations of these techniques which allow for the expression of any weaver's ideas.

The basic difference between traditional tapestry weaving and other kinds of weaving is the specific use of interlock and slit techniques. Tapestry techniques are used in several of the weaving methods described in previous chapters. These techniques can be combined with other techniques or employed throughout the entire weaving. When used for the entire design, cardboard or wood frames make practical devices for holding the warp.

Ryan Kidd, grade 3, lifts warp threads as he works on a tapestry project. The finished work is shown on page 61. Photo courtesy of Eileen Scally.

PREPARING A TAPESTRY FRAME

There are three basic methods for preparing a frame for weaving.

Method 1

The first method is to tie string to all pins. In this method, ordinary straight pins are inserted along the top and bottom edges of the frame. A string is tied around the first end-pin of the top row, gently pulled down, wrapped around the first end-pin of the bottom row, and tied. This procedure is followed for all the pins.

Method 2

The second method is to tie string to the first and last pins only. In the second method, the string is wrapped around all the pins and tied only to the first and last pin.

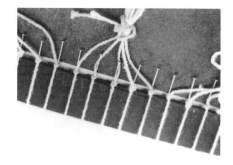

Method 3

The third method is to wrap the warp completely around the frame with slits in the cardboard anchoring the warp and keeping the strands vertical. When a wood frame is used, the warp is wrapped tightly so the strands will keep their position without anchoring.

Interlocking of color.

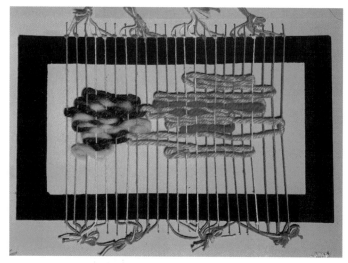

To prepare this frame for weaving, the weaver inserted ordinary straight pins along the top and bottom edges of the frame. Then the weaver tied string around the first end pin of the top row, and gently pulled the string down around the first end pin of the bottom row, continuing until there was string on all the pins.

Open areas using slit technique.

WEAVING PROCEDURE

Tapestry weaving employs the basic technique of linking areas of adjacent weft threads, which may be similar or different in color. This is done by: interlocking strands of single, double, or even triple threads; wrapping weft threads from two sections around the same warp thread; or turning the weft thread around separate warp strands, leaving open areas or slits between part of the pattern. To make a tapestry design, weave only partway across the warp, reversing the weaving direction of the weft thread at different points of the weaving process.

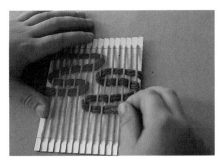

Interlock strands of single, double, or even triple threads.

Wrap weft threads from two different sections of the weaving around a single warp thread.

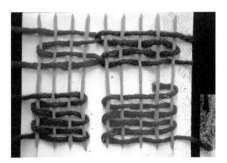

Leave open areas or slits between parts of the design.

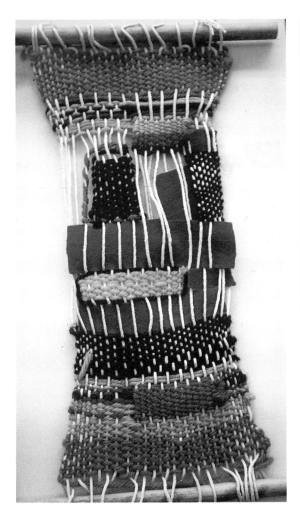

Student work, college.

Part of this weaving is made with tapestry techniques. Strips of felt add contrast to the weft.

Many weavers create their tapestry patterns by weaving spontaneously, while others make preplanned drawings. If you choose to make a drawing, you can use it as a guide or reference for weaving a design having one or many shapes. You can draw the shape (animal, person, or bird) in silhouette on a sheet of paper, using crayon or paint to plan the sections of color. Large areas of color work best. After you stretch the warp on a frame or cardboard, place your prepared design under the warp strands as a guide. It is easier to weave the shape first, then the background. Once you understand the basic procedure, you can explore different approaches to find the one that will serve you best as you apply the basic tapestry techniques discussed in the chapter.

Position your drawing under the warp threads.

Weave the main figure first, then the background.

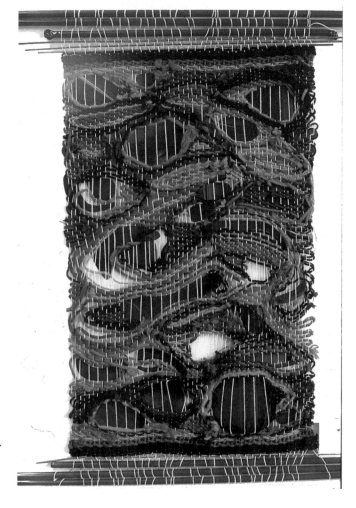

Colored celluloid has been woven into the warp as accent. The warp is held by glass rods at top and bottom.

This weaving uses the slit technique, interlocking strands, and linked areas of adjacent weft threads. It is so tightly woven, however, that these techniques are hard to see from a distance. Tapestry rug, 6 x 4' (18.3 x 12.2 m) by children of Harrania, Egypt. Collection of the author.

Weavers can push weft threads into wavy lines, and tie other warp threads to form a pattern.

Zigzag lines lead the viewer's eye to the solid figure. Student work, elementary.

VARIATIONS

These techniques can be combined
with tapestry weaving to produce
different textural effects.

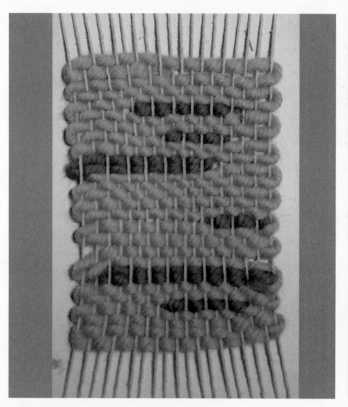

Inlay different colors within the weft.

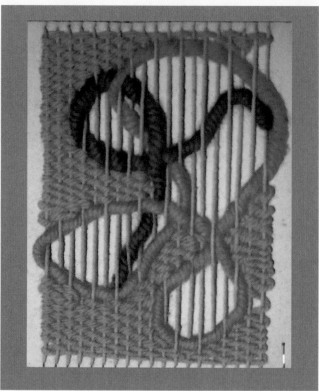

Use heavy weight yarns in conjunction with lighter weight
yarns.

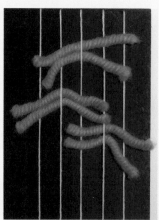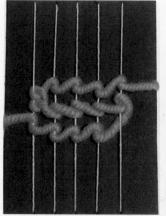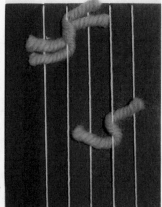

Techniques such as those shown in these photographs will help you vary the look of the weft.

Here, textured yarns have been interlocked using tapestry techniques. Parts of the warp have been tied, and inlaid weaving fills in other areas. The large bead makes an interesting focal point. Cassandra Lee Tellier, *Miniature*. Courtesy of the artist.

Threads in this tapestry, made by fifth grade children of Harrania, Egypt, are tightly woven together using three tapestry techniques. Collection of the author.

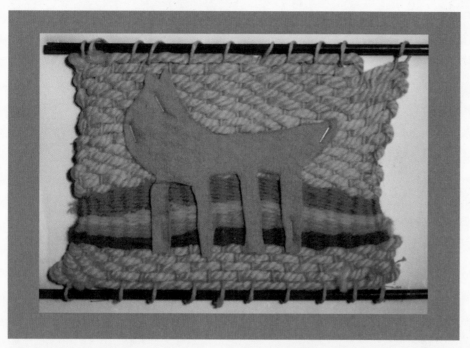

The student who made this tapestry weaving added a felt appliqué in an animal shape.

The contrast between tightly woven and loose areas in this tapestry helps create visual interest. Frequent color changes offer a challenge to the weaver.

A close-up shows the narrow warp threads and bulky weft yarns the artist used.

Interlocking of colors, threads, and open spaces.

13

Rug Hooking

Rug hooking, which is simple enough for children, employs a tool with a hooked end to pull and push yarn back and forth through a background material. It is effective when combined with weaving or stitchery; like weaving, it allows you to experience the excitement of working with smooth, rough, hard and soft yarns. Designing new and varied arrangements of color, texture, and pattern will challenge your ingenuity. The resulting works can range from shag effects to low relief sculpture, from inviting floor rugs to dramatic wall hangings.

Ideas for design are everywhere—a painting or print, cut-paper shapes, plant life viewed through a microscope, shapes of buildings, nature. All the endless visual patterns in our daily lives offer constant and changing sources.

Rug by Heidi G. Yates. Courtesy of the artist.

(opposite) Angela Bangrazi, *The Old Lady Who Swallowed a Fly.* Wool, 40" (102 cm) diameter. Courtesy of the artist.

PROCEDURE

To begin any rug or wall hanging, you can use one of two basic rug-hooking procedures. These procedures form the basis from which you can branch out and find your own approach through experimentation. The first method involves the use of a backing fabric and any one of three tools: the punch needle, shuttle hooker, or hand hook (a crochet needle can also be substituted for the hand hook). The second method makes use of a tool called the loop latch hook and a backing material of scrim.

Punch Needle Method

To use the punch needle and burlap or monk's cloth, decide on the rug size; then cut the fabric backing to that size, allowing several extra inches on each edge for a margin. Use a handmade frame of soft wood, a ready-made picture frame, or one of the specially designed stretcher or rug frames. Stretch the backing tightly over the frame and fasten it with staples or

(left) Large, simple designs work best for rug hooking.

(below) Use a loop gauge (top) to help keep the size of loops consistent.

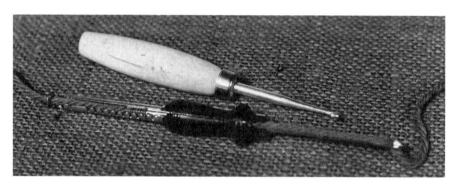

carpet tacks. Cut a piece of wrapping paper the size of the proposed rug. With crayon, felt-tip pen, or chalk, draw a bold design that will fill the space inside the margin. Avoid tiny detail and line drawings.

Transfer your design in one of these three ways: (1) sketch directly on the burlap with a felt-tip pen or charcoal, (2) paint a design on the burlap with dye, or (3) cut out the shape and use it as a pattern.

To use the hand hook, apply your design to the front of the burlap backing. Insert the hook through the backing to pull the yarn or cloth strips from the back to the front surface.

To use the punch needle, thread the yarn through the ring at the top of the handle and then through the inside point. Pull about a foot of yarn through the needle; then drag the yarn back,

Pierce the fabric from back to front.

Push until the handle touches the fabric.

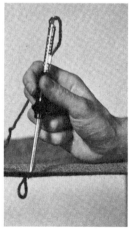

Pull the needle back.

Repeat to make additional loops.

Keep loops close together to create a tight weave.

George Wells, *Primitive Horse Rug*. Courtesy of The George Wells Ruggery.

with tension, so it will gradually slip into the tube and handle. Set the loop gauge for the length of loop you want. With the back side of the backing fabric facing up, push the needle through the backing until the needle's handle touches the backing fabric and creates a loop underneath, on the front side. Pull the needle back to the surface. Do not jerk, but glide it from one loop to another. Continue the process of punching the needle back and forth through the burlap. You can use one hand to insert the hook, while the other hand checks the loop length underneath. When you've completed a small amount of hooking, the loops will begin to hold one another tightly.

George Wells, *Leaf Rug*. Courtesy of The George Wells Ruggery.

The hooking technique makes a surface that has both visual and tactile appeal. You can create a variety of textures on this surface if you experiment with different treatments of the loops. For example, snipping the end of each loop will give the rug a velvety appearance. Try shearing the tops off the loops; sculpturing the loops to give the rug a low-relief effect; varying the length of loops, making some high and others low; combining clipped and unclipped loops; or combining yarn, strips of fabric or leather.

When all parts of the design are finished, remove the rug from the frame, then fold back the edges and stitch them to the back of the rug. Paint latex sizing over the back of the finished piece to give the rug body, hold the yarn securely in place, and prevent slipping if it is to be placed on the floor. If the rug is to be a wall hanging, sizing is not necessary.

Cut each loop to create a velvety look.

Snip off the tops of the loops.

Vary the length of the loops.

Add accents in leather or other materials.

Finish rug edges by folding back extra materials and tacking them down by stitching. Photo courtesy George Wells.

Loop Latch Hook Method

The loop latch hook, used when working with a scrim backing, knots the yarn into the backing. For this type of rug hooking, cut a piece of scrim, leaving enough material on all four sides to turn back for a finished edge. With a crayon, draw a design on paper to match the size of the rug. Place the paper under the scrim, and with a felt-tip pen trace the lines of the design on the material. This procedure is illustrated in Chapter 3. Because of its stiffness, scrim does not need to be placed on a frame.

Cut pieces of yarn the length desired, usually about two inches. To avoid interrupting the hooking process for constant cutting and measuring, prepare enough pieces at one time to complete a small section. Bring the two ends of yarn together and hold them between your fingers to form a loose loop. Put the hook through the loop and under one strand of the scrim. Pull the two ends of the yarn up to the point of the hook and place them between the hook and latch. Close the latch and pull the hook back through the scrim and also through the previous loop, holding the ends of yarn with fingers to form a knot in the yarn. Continue this process, keeping the loops close together.

This simple introduction to hooking techniques has merely scratched the surface of the wide range of possibilities suggested by this medium. Experiment and discover new avenues, new methods, and new combinations.

A loop latch hook with the latch open.

Put the latch hook through the loop of yarn and under one strand of scrim.

Pull the yarn ends up into the latch and close it.

Pull the hook back under the scrim and through the yarn loop.

The finished loop.

Jack Arends, *Rug*. Courtesy of the artist.

VARIATION

An unusual variation to the hooking technique is rug hooking at the easel. Attach a large piece of scrim to a wood frame, then place the frame on an easel, which serves only to hold the frame. Several weavers can work simultaneously, each making a design for a particular area of the piece. This group approach to rug hooking enables each weaver to see his or her design emerge, as each shape becomes a part of the finished piece.

RUG KNOTTING

The Ghiordes Knot

The Ghiordes knot (sometimes called the symmetrical knot or Turkish knot) is named for a town in northwest Turkey. To make this knot, the weft thread is looped over two warp threads, and both ends of the loop emerge between the warp threads, creating the carpet's pile. This versatile knot may be combined with weaving or knotted to a coarsely woven backing material.

To make loops of equal size, place the yarn strand under a horizontal rod before pulling it through the background material. This will serve as a gauge for loop strengths.

Close-up of Ghiordes knots in a cardboard weaving.

Beginning of a loop.

View of the loop as it is being pulled down to form a knot.

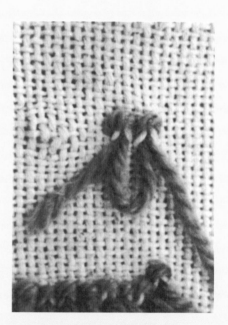

The yarn has been pulled tight to form a knot. As a new knot is started, a loop is left at the bottom. The entire design may be made with cut or uncut loops.

Abby Vakay, *Lake View*, hooked and tufted mixed fiber, plus molten glass, 16 x 20" (41 x 51cm). Courtesy of the artist.

Abby Vakay, *Ken Kesey Dream*, hooked and tufted mixed fiber, 24 x 18" (61 x 46 cm). Courtesy of the artist.

14

OTHER IMAGINATIVE
Ideas and Techniques

There are several ways to give students the experience of weaving without actually using weaving materials. Crayoned lines, for example, can function just as threads do, and can be woven over and under one another. Drawings of this kind can also be used to plan actual weavings.

Crayoned lines suggest a variety of weaving techniques.

(opposite) An example of needle weaving with string: The warp was stretched at unequal points around the frame; the weft was woven with a large needle, creating irregular spaces and textures. Collection of the author.

WEAVING WITH UNLIKELY MATERIALS

Is there anything you can't use to make a weaving? Of course there is, but you'll find several unexpected raw materials here. Look them over, and then start to think of your own unusual combinations.

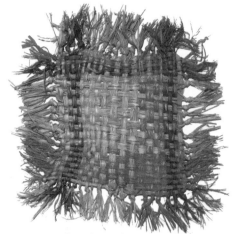

Warp and weft made with raffia. Courtesy of Rachel Sullivan.

Wheat woven into flat reed. Student work, grade 1. Courtesy of Joan Foucht, Columbus, Ohio.

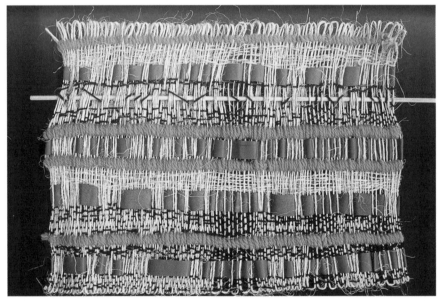

Combine wide strips of leather or fabric with thin yarns and dowel for contrast.

Materials from nature offer rich weaving possibilities. Here, corn husks, fungi, alfalfa, weeds, barley, and cattails mingle harmoniously.

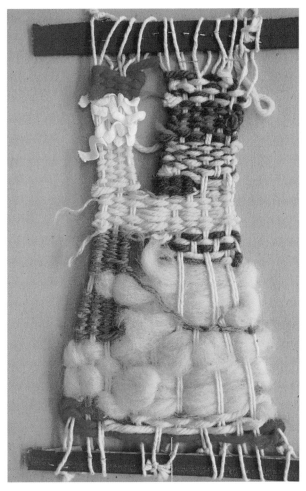

Raw cotton used for the weft contrasts sharply with thinner threads.

(right) Cassandra Lee Tellier, *Tampa's Shoes*. Leather, 11 x 22" (28 x 56 cm). Courtesy of the artist.

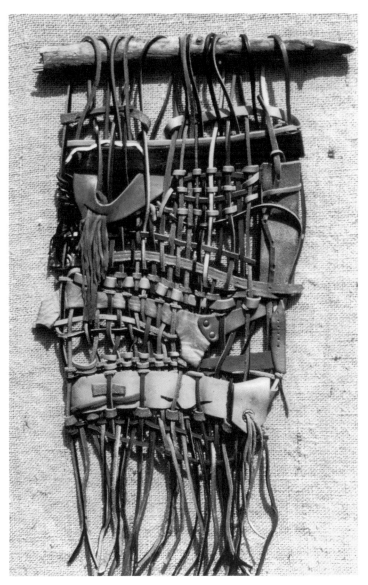

Bamboo snowflake. Collection of Joan Foucht, Columbus, Ohio.

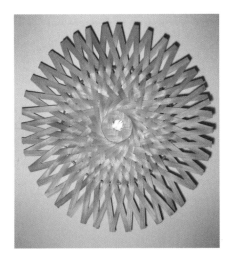

Woven bamboo. Collection of Kelly and Richard Hughes, Naples, Florida.

More Unlikely Materials

Cassandra Lee Tellier, *Return to Africa*. Wood, jute, feathers, weeds, 19 x 25" (48 x 64 cm). Courtesy of the artist.

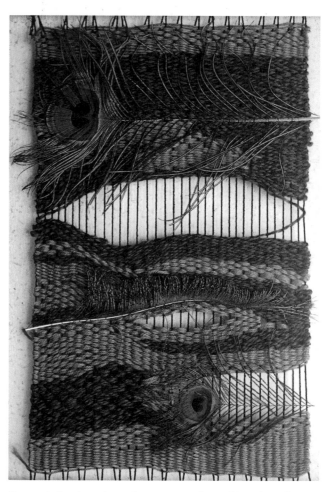

Peacock feathers have been woven into this otherwise traditional yarn weaving. Author, 18 x 24" (46 x 61 cm).

These baskets were made by wrapping yarn over a core of welting rope. Looped leather strips (left) and looped yarn cut into fringe (right) have been added as accents.

JEWELRY

Weaving offers many inventive opportunities to the process of jewelry making. Interesting creations can be made of fibers, fabric, string, natural materials such as dried weeds and flower stems, as well as strips of metal and strands of wire of various gauges. You can weave and interlace wire on wire armatures, or use leather, fur, and fabric that compliment articles of clothing. Jewelry variations can be added to purses or used to adorn woven sculptures.

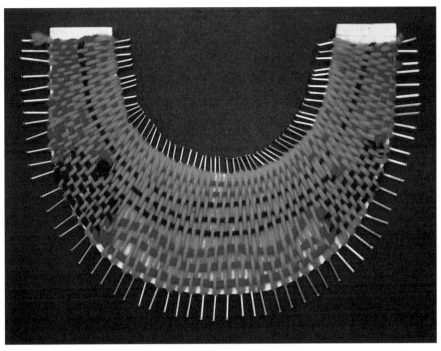

This yarn neck piece was made on a piece of cardboard. Straight pins held the yarn in place; when the weaving was complete, the edges were stitched to hold their shape. Yarn can be wrapped around pins or around both sides of the cardboard. If the neckpiece is woven on one side only, the cardboard can be bent to remove it and the pins from the weaving.

Reed has been incorporated as part of this neckpiece, which was woven on cardboard.

Each of the three parts of this necklace was woven separately on cardboard.

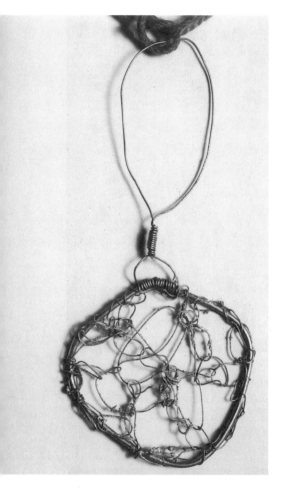

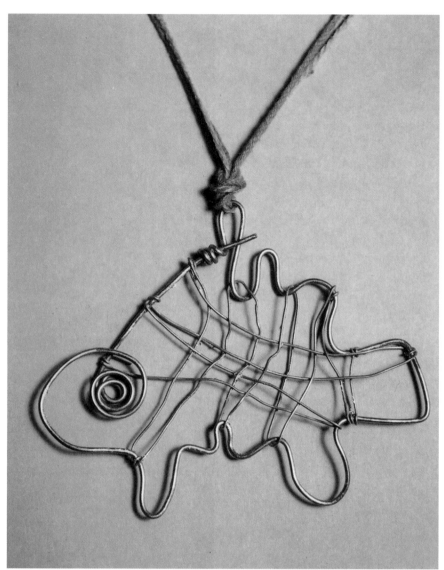

(above left) Wire was wrapped around a bent wire outline, woven and interlocked to form a lacy pattern. Use a crochet hook to create lacy effects with very fine gauge wire. (above) Heavy gauge wire was shaped, then lighter wire was used to create warp and weft inside the shape. (left) Small dowels, reed, or twigs give woven jewelry body and help hold the shape flat.

GOD'S EYE OR STRING CROSS

Apparently originating with the Huichol tribe of Jalisco, Mexico, the God's Eye is a simple weaving made using two sticks. In traditional Mexican families, fathers weave a God's Eye each time a child is born, and add another width of yarn or string for each year of the child's life until the age of five.

Procedure

To make a God's Eye weaving, choose twigs or branches of equal size to be used for the base or beginning of the design. To fasten the twigs together, glue or twist wire or a rubber band around the center. It is also possible to hold the twigs together with yarn glued to one twig before starting.

Wrap the yarn around one twig, and then extend the yarn over to the twig to the right or left. Avoid crossing strands over one another. Make your design on both the front and back of the weaving. Experiment to find ways that work best for you.

Continue to span the space between the twigs with strands of yarn. Change colors for more interest.

Back and front of God's Eyes made of craft sticks. Courtesy Victoria Bedford Betts.

BASIC MATERIALS
twigs, branches, ice cream sticks
scissors
adhesive (especially good is rubber cement or tri-tex paste)
yarn

Optional Materials
toothpicks
lollipop sticks
bamboo sticks
wire from coat hangers
dowel rods
flat craft or ice cream sticks
yarns of various kinds including angora and mohair

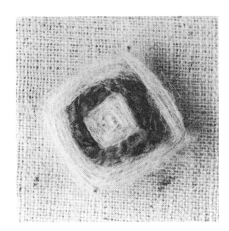

Change colors and textures to create more interest.

You can use twigs or branches as a base.

Form a cross.

Wrap yarn over and under the twigs to hold them in place. Glue the yarn to the first twig if necessary.

Wrap yarn around one twig, and then stretch it across to the nearest twig to the left or right.

VARIATIONS

God's Eyes are very popular in Mexico and Peru. In the contemporary world this old technique offers new directions for exploration.

- To vary the technique, use a more intricate twig or put two twigs together.
- Group several God's Eyes vertically and horizontally to form a design.
- Attach them to a backing with glue and suspend them as a mobile or a wall hanging.
- Make other mobiles by suspending the God's Eyes from a dowel or coat hanger.
- Superimpose the God's Eyes against a burlap background or incorporate them in a weaving.
- Fasten twigs together to make a three-dimensional form which, with yarn woven around it, will give a sculptural, cobweb effect that is artistic as well as unusual.

God's Eye Totem, British Columbia, Canada. Collection of the author.

God's Eye variation. Two branches taped together form the basic structure. Wrapped and knotted yarn was stretched in different directions to form warp and weft.

Author, *God's Eye Composition*. Mohair.

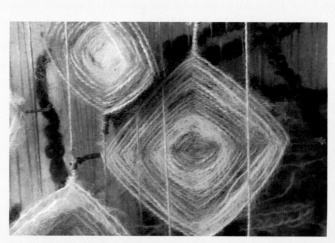

Author, *God's Eye Composition*, detail.

NEEDLEPOINT VARIATION

Scrim, discussed in Chapter 3, makes a good background for needlepoint. Customarily needlepoint stitches are made in one direction but, even with a frame, this results in some distortion of the scrim backing. To avoid this distortion, make the stitches in two directions as shown in the rug example. This technique opens new areas of exploration for the designer.

Needlepoint by Lydia Bancroft. Courtesy of the artist.

A VARIATION OF KNITTING

This process produces a weave that looks very like the knitting technique used to create ribbing on cuffs and hems.

To begin, make a rectangular wood frame with horizontal pieces about 8 inches (20 cm) long. If you wish the knitting to be wider, make the horizontal pieces longer. Cut and nail two end pieces to hold the frame together, leaving a 2-inch (5 cm) space between the horizontal pieces. This will allow the knitting to slip through the center as the interlocked yarn increases in length. Hammer nails about ½ inch (1.2 cm) apart along the horizontal wood to attach the yarn.

1. Knot the yarn around the first top nail on the left.

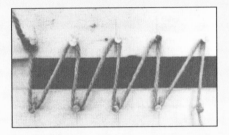

2. Pull the yarn down and around the bottom nail; up, over, and around the second top nail, and so on. Continue winding the yarn this way until all the nails have been used.

3. Begin to wind the yarn back toward the left end of the slot. As you wind the yarn over the nails, pull the bottom strand up, over, and off the nail to form a loop.

4. Continue this process for each nail.

5. As the weaving progresses, the work slips through the opening between the nails in the frame.

With this process, you can vary the knitted patterns by winding the yarn several times around the same nail or different nail combinations.

15

PROVOCATIVE Variations

There are many ways to make your weavings inspiring and unique. Experiment with a wide variety of materials and techniques and you're bound to come up with meaningful and thought-provoking combinations.

Denna M. Donley, *Double Swirl*. Gourd, woven sweet grass. Courtesy of the artist.

(right) Tie-dyed raffia cloth interlaced into a seamless tube without the use of a loom. Dida, Ivory Coast. © Werner Forman/Art Resource, NY

(opposite) Sally J. Bright, *Together They Move Like Liquid*. Reed. Courtesy of the artist.

PAPER

Although paper is the simplest of materials, and generally the most plentiful in the classroom, don't underestimate its potential when you're considering complex woven works. The examples shown here should convince you that artists of any age or ability can be challenged by paper weaving.

Warp-Dominated Design

To make complex paper weavings, cut an intricate design from thin tag board as a guide for creating the warp. Trace the guide multiple times across a sheet of sturdy paper, and use an X-acto knife to cut out the design. Weave straight strips of paper through the warp, varying color, texture, and material to create additional interest.

Sculptural Weave

There are many ways to manipulate the paper you use in a weaving. Try combining several paper sculpture techniques to create a dynamic, heavily textured weaving.

- Cut a straight warp, and remove every other warp strip.
- Place a second sheet of paper under the initial warp, and cut thin warp strips in that second sheet. The strips should be visible through the open areas of the first sheet of paper.
- To create a three-dimensional effect, fold and crease paper strips used as weft. The bulk of the folded strips will raise the warp and create interesting shadows and highlights.

Weave straight strips of paper through the warp. Vary paper colors to create interest. Courtesy Fern Szabo, Naples, Florida.

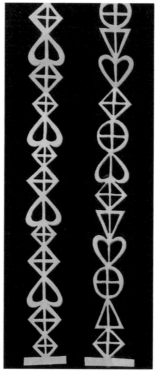

Cut an intricate design from a strip of thin tag board. Courtesy Fern Szabo, Naples, Florida.

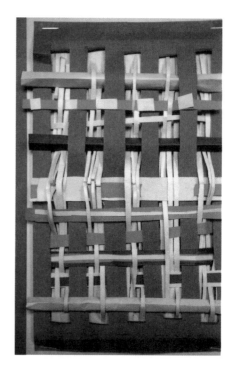

A double warp plus varied weft strips—some three-dimensional, some of different colors and widths—results in a highly textured overall effect. Courtesy of Eileen Scally.

NEEDLE WEAVE

Procedure

1. Using a wooden frame or notched cardboard, stretch warp threads vertically from top to bottom.

2. Next, stretch threads horizontally across the frame or cardboard.

3. Stretch threads at a slant from top left to bottom right.

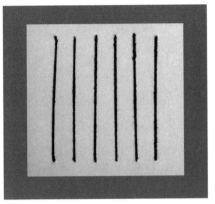

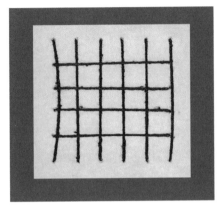

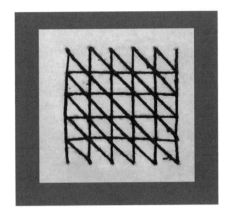

Photos courtesy of Linda Panitz Costello

4. Stretch threads from the top right to the bottom left.

5. Create a second set of vertical strands over the horizontal and slanted strands. Position this set of strands evenly between the first set of vertical strands.

6. Using a needle, weave under the intersection of each X-shaped figure; then make a stitch by looping the yarn back over the same intersection. Continue, making a stitch around each X-shaped intersection. On alternate rows, weave over and under, but do not loop.

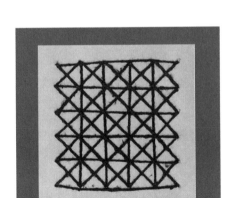

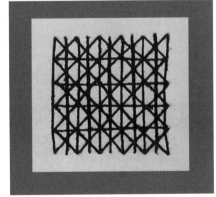

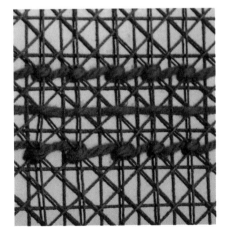

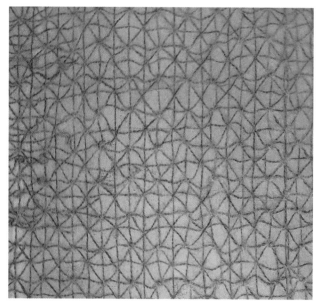

The result of the needle weave procedure is a loosely-woven, airy fabric.

Dowels punctuate this delicate wall hanging.

THE WOVEN TRIANGLE

The simple woven triangle is an example of how warp threads may also be used as weft threads. The outside warp thread of one edge is woven under and over the remaining warp. The outside thread of the opposite side is then used for weaving. As the warp threads decrease in number, the weft threads increase. This process is repeated until all warp threads have been woven as weft, resulting in a triangle.

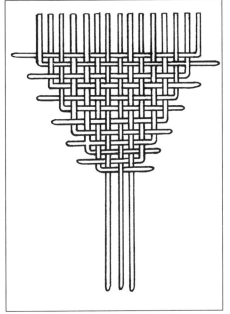

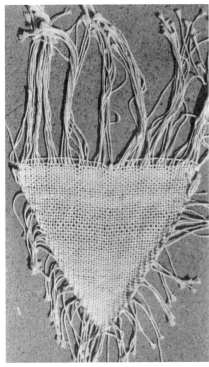

As the warp threads decrease in number, the weft threads increase, creating a triangle. Courtesy Connie Ward.

THE SLIT

While the slit is a traditional technique, it can offer an added dimension to the weaving process. One way to make the slit is to fasten a wire to any two warp threads which may later form the slit; then complete the weaving and bend the wire into a pleasing shape. Another method is to allow for the slit as the weaving progresses, then weave a piece of wire through the threads around the edge of the slit.

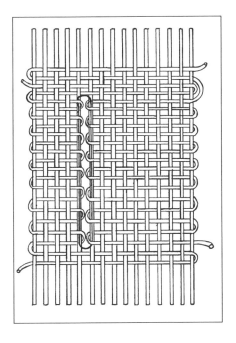

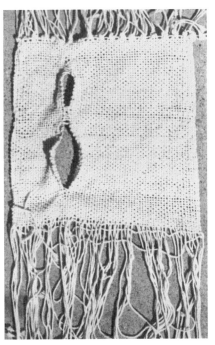

Weaving wire around the edges of the slit allows you to shape the slit as you wish when the weaving is finished. Courtesy Connie Ward.

A FORM WOVEN ON A BRANCH

A creative weaver can see possibilities in the simplest devices. Even an ordinary tree branch—like those used as looms by primitive peoples—can inspire the imaginative person to try new and exciting techniques.

Follow these steps for this technique:

1. Knot two warp strands together at one end and place one strand on each side of the branch; then bring the two threads together and knot. This keeps the warp in the proper position on the branch.
2. Continue fastening the warp in strands of two around the branch until there is enough for weaving.
3. Suspend the branch to permit the warp threads to hang freely during the weaving process.
4. Attach weights to the bottom ends of the warp, thereby providing greater tension.

In the example shown here, the warp is arranged so that a cylinder is formed first. Gradually eliminating warp threads by weaving them as weft creates a conical shape.

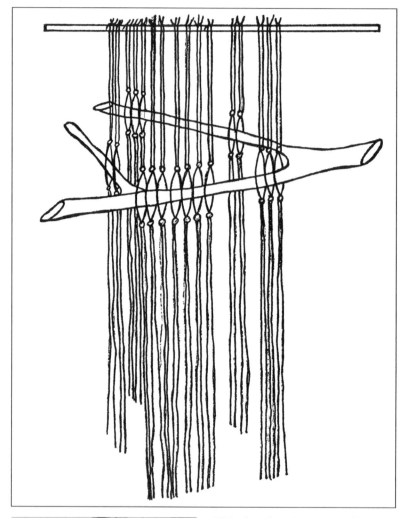

This drawing shows how knots above and below each branch help keep the warp threads in position. Courtesy Connie Ward.

OTHER POSSIBILITIES

Work with sculptural forms, add calligraphy or printing—there are innumerable ways to make your weavings unique.

Honma Kazuaki, *Sound of Waves II*, 2000. Hobichiku and kurochiku bamboos, using Mage and hineri-ami technique, 19 x 22 x 17½" high (49 x 56 x 43 cm). Courtesy TAI Gallery, Santa Fe, NM.

To make this woven form, the artists painted sheets of aluminum with acrylics. The sheets were cut into strips, and the artists wove the strips over a wooden framework. James Mosier and Wendy Benard, *Woven Aluminum Vessel*. Courtesy of the artists.

Thin strips of metal and wire were interwoven to form this basket. Collection of the author.

The woven glass sculptures below began as sand, which was heated and cooled precisely, handwoven as molten glass, fired as many as four times at temperatures of up to 1500°F, and then fire polished over handmade molds.

Eric Markow and Thom Norris, *Confetti*, 2005. AP/50. Woven and annealed glass, 19 x 19 x 5" (48 x 48 x 13 cm). Photograph by Javier Agostinelli.

Bonnie Eastwood, *Gourd*. Seaweed woven on gourd, with reed base. Paper collage accent on front. Courtesy of the artist.

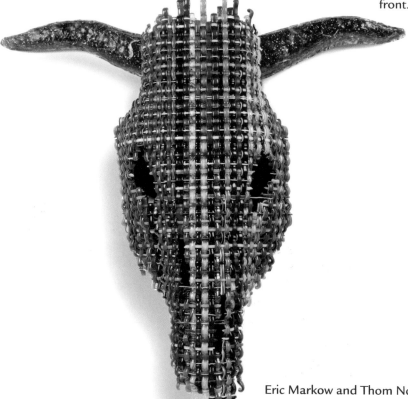

Eric Markow and Thom Norris, *Santa Fe Skull*, 2006. AP/15. Woven and annealed glass, 27 x 25 x 7" (69 x 64 x 18 cm). Photograph by Javier Agostinelli.

Woven Combinations

mind is a weaver,

winding threads of gold and gray

on the loom of a day

heart is the spinner

catching the stuff of joy and sorrow

onto quills

for tomorrow.

Calligraphy is combined here with woven lines and small printed shapes on a background fabric. Collection of the author.

Gina Skillings, Stoneware teapot with reed handle and woven yarn detail. The artist made vertical cuts in the side of this teapot while the clay was still wet. She then fired the pot and wove yarn through the cuts, creating a lush, furry look. Courtesy of the artist.

16

TEXTURES AND Weaves

The act of weaving creates textures, and the texture of a weaving may be one of the first characteristics you notice. Texture may be tactile or visual. Tactile texture allows you to touch and feel roughness or smoothness, such as that found in burlap, rope, cloth, fur, carpet, or yarns. In addition to the textures of the materials themselves, you can also manipulate your materials, creating loops and knots, or wrapping and clipping fibers to form textures.

Visual texture resembles real texture. Photographs or drawings of carpet, thick and thin yarns, tree bark, beads, or other fibers can be used to create visual substitutes for real texture.

(opposite) Peacock feathers add a texture unlike any that yarn can provide. Artwork by the author.

(right) Shells and pipe cleaners have been woven into the warp.

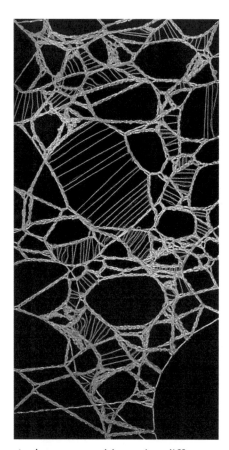

String used as warp and yarn as weft have been superimposed over a background of cut paper and oil pastel.

Author, composition using different sized weaving yarns and crochet techniques.

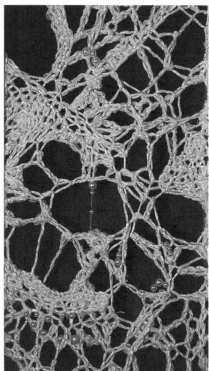

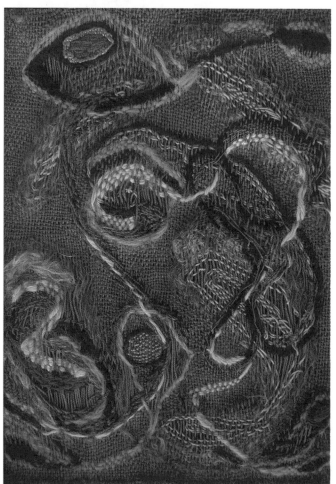

Author, composition using weaving and crochet. Iridescent yarns, 8 x 13" (20 x 33 cm).

Stitchery superimposed on weaving.

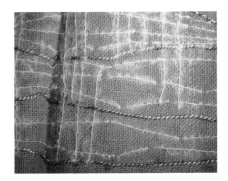

Mohair and gold cord woven into burlap.

Cassandra Lee Tellier, *Holidays*. Wool and synthetic fibers, 11 x 15" (28 x 38 cm). Courtesy of the artist.

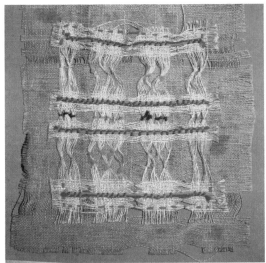

The artist removed warp and weft threads from the bottom layer of burlap, then did the same on another, lighter-colored layer, and used colorful yarn to stitch them together.

In these weavings, the artists have formed textures by creating open spaces. Slubs in the yarn also add textured areas.

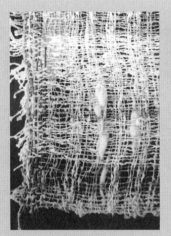

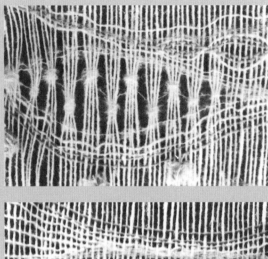

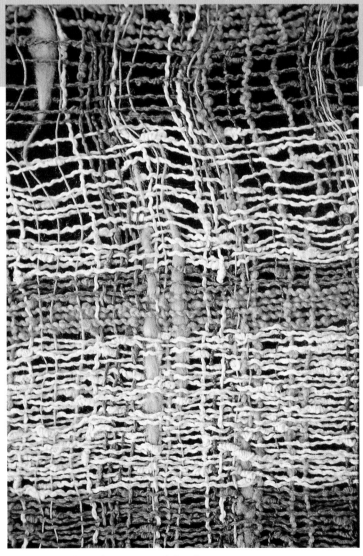

Nubby silk threads were used for this warp.

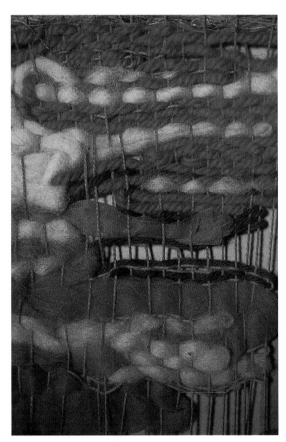

Nylon stockings combine well with traditional yarn, creating wider areas of weft.

Crisp jute and fibrous mohair are used together in this design.

Notice the pieces of carpet used as weft at the top and bottom of this weaving.

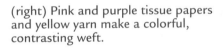

(right) Pink and purple tissue papers and yellow yarn make a colorful, contrasting weft.

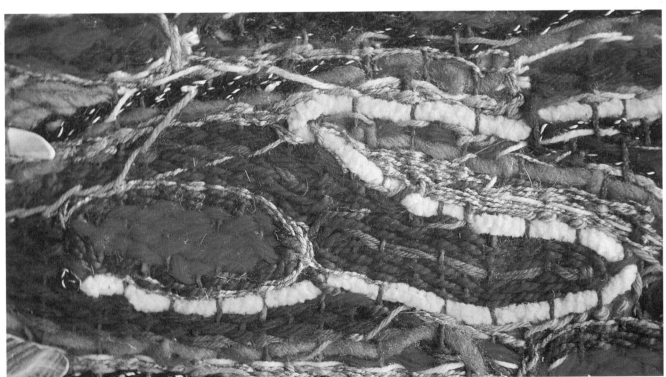

Pipe cleaners create a wandering line in yellow.

In all these cardboard weavings, variations in the pattern help create texture.

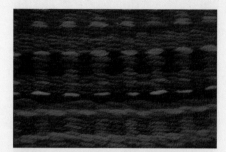

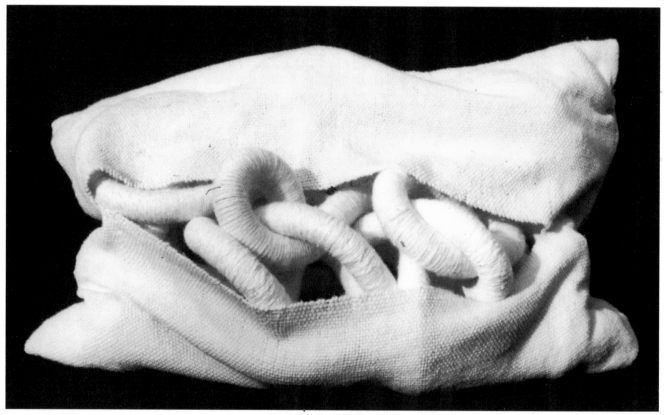

Cassandra Lee Tellier, *Sack of Tubes*. Courtesy of the artist.

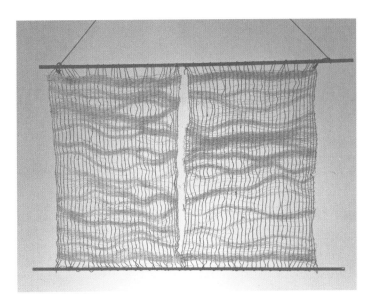

Author, wall hanging. Linen threads used as weft and warp. 25 x 30" (64 x 76 cm).

Sheila Hicks, © Copyright *Greta Weaving (no. 55)*. Wool, 9 x 5¾". Photo: Digital Image © The Museum of Modern Art/Licensed by SCALA / Art Resource, NY

17

WOVEN Forms

Although weavings are often thought of as flat, rectangular shapes, woven forms are intricate shapes in three dimensions. Expanding your thinking to suspension in space adds another approach to creative weaving. Warp strands can be attached to rods, tree branches, and other natural found structures. Mixed media, including plaster, wood, or wire, can form still other structures. Adding tactile objects such as beads, feathers, leather and the like will create more color and interest.

Gloria Roberts, *Peaceful Night*. Woven background with coiled trees, 72 x 48" (183 x 122 cm). Courtesy of the artist.

(opposite) Gloria Roberts, *Beautiful Day*. Woven background with coiled tree, 52 x 52" (132 x 132 cm). Courtesy of the artist.

In this work, the artist pulled threads through pierced holes in a tree branch. A large stone serves as a weight to hold the form straight. Student work, college.

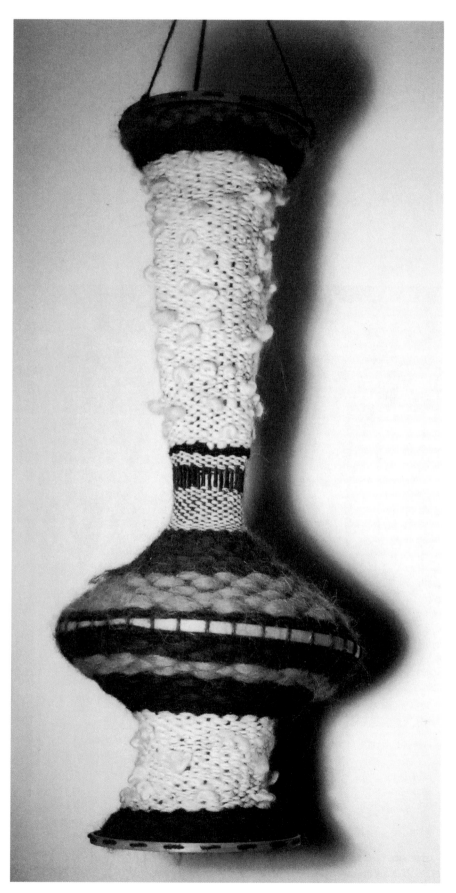

Hanging form. Collection of author.

Woven wall hanging by author.

Author, *Puppet Man*. Variegated yarns, 12 x 28" (30 x 71 cm).

GLOSSARY

bye-spokes Extra spokes inserted beside the first spokes to strengthen the weaving.

canvas stretcher Strips of wood fitted together to form a frame. Small triangles are inserted at corners to make frame sturdy.

collage A design or picture made by pasting an arrangement of materials on a background.

cross-stitch canvas A coarse, starched-like cloth usually woven in a regular mesh. May be used for tapestry, embroidery or rug hooking. Sometimes called scrim.

dowel rods Wooden rods used for hanging finished work. They may be inserted through the warp threads of the weaving, or the top of the weaving may be lapped over the rod.

God's Eye A small cross, often made of twigs or branches, with colored yarn or thread wound around in the shape of a square set in a diagonal position.

loop latch hook A tool with a hook and latch at one end, set in a wooden handle.

latex sizing A liquid rubber used for painting the back of a hooked rug.

low-relief A sculptural form in which portions of the design protrude slightly from the background.

monoprint One print, made by creating a design with ink or paint on a surface, then placing fabric or paper on top of the design. Rubbing over the paper or fabric transfers the design.

pairing Using two reeds at the same time, twisting with each reed alternately.

punch needle A tool with a gauge for setting length of loop. Used for hooking technique.

randing In basketry, the over-and-under weave, in front of one stake and behind the next, with a single reed. It is best to have an uneven number of stakes for this weave.

rug hook Similar to a crochet hook set in a wood handle; used for rug hooking.

scrim A fabric often used as backing for rug hooking. Sometimes called cross-stitch canvas.

spokes Reeds that radiate from the center of the base of a basket form.

stakes The upright reeds which form the foundation upon which the basket sides are woven.

stitchery Various types of stitches combined to form a design.

structural skeleton The arrangement of warp threads.

tabby A simple pattern developed by weaving over and under alternate threads.

tapestry A type of over-and-under weaving, employing the basic tapestry technique of linking adjacent weft threads which may be similar or different in color.

taut Tightly drawn threads or fabric.

waling The use of three strands of reed woven in a twined effect.

warp A series of threads that lie in a vertical position.

weft Horizontal threads or fibers used for weaving over-and-under the warp.

BIBLIOGRAPHY

Alderman, Sharon D., *Mastering Weave Structures*. Loveland, CA: Interweave Press, Inc., 2004.

Black, Mary E., *The Key to Weaving*. New York: Macmillan, 1980.

Coffland, Robert T., *Contemporary Japanese Bamboo Arts*. Art Media Resources, Chicago, 2000.

Cotsen, Lloyd and Robert T. Coffland, *The Bamboo Basket Art of Higashi Takesonosai*. Art Media Resources, Chicago, 2002.

Coffland, Robert T. and Donald Doe, *Hin: The Quiet Beauty of Japanese Bamboo Art*. Art Media Resources, Chicago. 2006.

Forman, W. and B., and Ramses Wissa Wassef, *Tapestries From Egypt*. Hamlyn House, UK: 1968.

Held, Shirley E., *Weaving: A Handbook of the Fiber Arts*. New York: Harcourt Brace, 1998.

LaFerla, Jane, *Making the New Baskets*. Asheville, NC: Lark Books, 1999.

Monaghan, Kathleen and Hermon Joyner, *You Can Weave*. Worcester, MA: Davis Publications, 2000.

Roth, Henry Ling, *Studies In Primitive Looms*: Halifax, UK: Bankfield Museum, 1950.

Sentance, Bryan, *Basketry: A World Guide to Traditional Techniques*. New York: Thames & Hudson, 2007.

ACKNOWLEDGMENTS

I wish to express my appreciation to school and university colleagues and friends who have offered their time and help during the preparation of the second edition of this book. I also wish to thank Dr. Louis Traina, Vice-President of Hodges University, Naples, Florida; Molly Weber, Computer Specialist; Claire Mowbray Golding, Editor; Dr. Warren L. Heltsley, Continuing Education, Edison College, Naples, Florida; and Dr. Jane Dorgan, Educational Consultant, Portsmouth, New Hampshire.

This book is dedicated to Scruffy, Ping, and Pong, for their patience while waiting for me to pet them.

INDEX